BEYOND THE LOVE GAME

BEYOND

THE

LOVE GAME

An Inner Guide to Finding Your Mate

ROBERT SCHEID

CELESTIAL ARTS
MILLBRAE, CALIFORNIA

We are grateful to the following for permission to quote from the works listed.

To Prentice-Hall, for permission to quote from *Executive ESP*, by Dean et al., (out of print). To Bantam Books, Inc., for permission to quote from *New Mind, New Body*, by Barbara B. Brown, Ph.D. All rights reserved. To Atesons/Richard L. Evans, Jr., for permission to quote from *The Richard Evans Quote Book*, by Richard L. Evans. To Fleming H. Revell Company, for permission to quote from *As a Man Thinketh*, by James Allen. To Unity School of Christianity for permission to quote from *Atom-Smashing Power of the Mind* and *Dynamics for Living*, by Charles Fillmore. To George C. Morris, representing Annalee Skarin, for permission to quote from *Celestial Song of Creation*, *Temple of God*, *To God the Glory*, and *Ye Are Gods*, by Annalee Skarin. To Deseret Books and Stephen R. Covey for permission to quote from *The Spiritual Roots of Human Relations*, by Stephen R. Covey. To Arthur James Limited for permission to quote from *Love Can Open Prison Doors*, by Starr Daily. To Tyndale House Publishers for permission to quote from *Magnificent Marriage*, by Gordon MacDonald.

Celestial Arts
231 Adrian Road
Millbrae, California 94030

First Printing, August 1980

Cover photograph by
Mike Powers

Cover design by Abigail Johnston

Made in the United States of America

Library of Congress Cataloging in Publication Data

Scheid, Robert, 1945–
    Beyond the love game..

    1. Interpersonal relations.   2. Love.   I. Title.
HM132.S35   158'.2   79-53839
ISBN 0-89087-254-6

1 2 3 4 5 6 7 — 86 85 84 83 82 81 80

PREFACE

*By all means marry; if you get a good
wife you'll become happy; if you get a
bad one you'll become a philosopher.*
                                              SOCRATES

SOCRATES had a good point. The problems of relationships between men and women have puzzled us for a very
long time. I'm sure all of us have either seen or heard of beautiful relationships that continually grow and expand without
becoming stale or empty. On the other hand, we have all
seen marriages or relationships that seemed outwardly perfect, but suddenly fell apart without any apparent reason.
One man, well-known for his research into the mind, remarked that he and his wife had a very good relationship,
but he did not exactly know why. What is it that makes one
relationship or marriage succeed and another fail?

In talking to, and reading about, people who have good relationships, I have found that most of them acknowledged
that something greater than themselves had brought them together. They felt that the success of their relationship was not
due to the use of certain techniques supposedly guaranteed to

make a relationship work. Religious beliefs were not seen as the binding force, either; religion sometimes bound people together, but not always out of love—it was sometimes a common mental belief or even fear! Having such things in common as background, interests, age, wealth, or even race did not seem to be essential. It appeared to be something deeper within these individuals that bound them together. It was something within the hearts of these individuals that made them one, and if a relationship did not have that essential ingredient it ceased to be truly happy.

When I moved to California in 1974 to become an instructor for Silva Mind Control, I began to understand what binds people to one another, and the more I thought about it, the simpler it became. Invariably people in my classes asked questions about their relationships. Some wondered why their relationship had suddenly fallen apart, sometimes from one day to the next. Others had become frustrated after going through one relationship after another without success. Many had no one at all—only a deep longing within them to be with the right person—and their question was "How do I attract the right person for me?" To many, desiring to be with the right person seemed to be a matter of survival; it was a subject which dominated much of their lives and thought.

It was then that I began to formulate ideas for a workshop designed to help participants attract the right person—their heart's desire, not just a suitable mate. I divided the workshop into two sections. The first half would deal with the mind and how it can help or hinder us in our relationships. Next I separated the mind into three distinct levels—the conscious mind, the subconscious mind, and the superconscious mind—in order to understand it more fully.

The conscious outer mind, for example, is the logical or intellectual mind. It is the mind we are taught to use in school, to the neglect of our other levels, to make all of our decisions. However, an amazing thing about this logical mind is that it was never intended, nor has it the capacity, to make decisions. In our Western society we have delegated to it a responsibility that it cannot handle. In the workshop one would learn the true purpose of the conscious mind and how to use it correctly, especially in relationships.

The next level is the subconscious mind, which is the realm of habit and emotions. This mind contains all of our experiences; it is like a giant hall of records, a huge memory bank. It is often compared rightly to a computer. People in relationships are often controlled by patterns in the subconscious mind. The workshop shows how important it is for people to understand these patterns and to let them go.

The third level of the mind, and the most profound, is the superconscious mind. This is the level where a true relationship takes place. It is the spark of divinity within us—the still, small voice; it is also the place where true knowing and understanding begin. By coming to understand each of these levels we gain valuable insight into the workings of our most intimate relationships.

From an understanding of how the mind operates, the workshop moves into its second half: How to attract the right person, and what goes into a true and loving relationship. The first topic to be discussed is communication and how we learn to listen, see, feel, and hear with the heart or soul. Honesty becomes important not only in coming from the heart but also in truly knowing ourselves.

The next topic is love, the basis of all life. Much has been written about love, but very little is said about the exact nature of love, what it is. People need to know about the transforming power of love, its ability to take any misfortune, heartbreak or failure and transmute it into love. Workshop participants learn how to use two other aspects of this divine love, gratitude and forgiveness, in their lives. We then talk about sexual relationships, and how making love relates to the physical, mental and spiritual aspects of our being.

The final topic is how to attract the right person and includes examples of people who have taken the workshop and have found the right person. I purposely save this subject for last because I feel people need to understand how their minds work and what goes into a true relationship before learning how to attract that special person.

In the four years that I have been presenting my workshop in the San Francisco Bay Area, I have found that people who sincerely and consistently apply the concepts of the workshop with their hearts and not with their intellects do get results. Unfortunately, some who take the workshop expected the workshop itself to bring them the right person, and, of course, it does not. These people usually fade back into their old patterns holding onto their frustrations and disappointments.

The concepts of the workshop must be taken into the heart and soul, and there understood and applied. Some of those who have applied the concepts have become personal friends, and I have seen their growth and their excitement at meeting the right person. This has been deeply gratifying. And I must add that everything taught in the workshops is true—I have used these concepts in my own life and I know that they work.

Since beginning to give the workshop, I have refined some of the concepts and have added others and I now feel ready to express them in a book. It is my profound desire that you who read the book will receive the same benefits as those taking the workshop.

CONTENTS

Dedicated . . .
To those who have loved and are willing
        to love again;
To those who earnestly and sincerely seek
        to do what is just and true;
To those who are willing to live by their hearts;
And God, our Creator, who is
        our Source.

I am deeply grateful to the many people who have helped in the divine unfoldment of the book: to David Patrick whose ideas and inspiration formed the basis of what later became a book; to Dorothy Grey whose encouragement and advice have been invaluable; to Helga, who was an answer to prayer; to Marcie Walburn, who, as God's instrument, graciously took time to spiritually sense the truthfulness of the manuscript; to Helen McGrath whose resourcefulness and knowing have helped the book to become a reality; to Barbara who lovingly typed the manuscript; to all those who took the workshops and classes which provided much of the material for the book; and to all those whose smiles and open hearts have meant encouragement along the way.

INTRODUCTION

IT BEGAN ON A COLD DAY in January. As I lay in bed that morning thoughts raced through my mind and I realized that a decision had to be made. The night's sleep had not changed anything, it had only been an escape from what I knew I had to face sooner or later.

I wanted to get up but my body would not move. I forced myself to sit up, then swung my feet to the floor and stood up. I remained there motionless, immobile. I took a deep breath, but it did not help. Every cell in my body seemed to ache and cry out for an answer, a release.

No, I did not have some terrible physical disease which was destroying my body; nor did I have an emotional problem which made me neurotic or something worse. Physical pain can at times overwhelm the body and mind and destroy them; mental anguish can be just as destructive. But the anguish I felt that morning went much deeper than physical or emotional pain. It went to the depths of my soul, and involved life itself. It was a longing, an unfulfilled longing deep within my heart that each cell in my body felt and experienced. It was not a fantasy or a wish for something material, but something so deep that only an open heart could comprehend and understand such a desire.

It was a longing to be with the right woman. The longing in my heart was not because I was sexually frustrated or because I was lonely and needed companionship. It was the desire to be with a special woman, the woman who would be right for me and for whom I would be right. I desired that oneness and completeness, that sense of belonging, that goes with being with the right woman. I knew that my life without her was incomplete and that I needed her to help me complete my purposes upon this earth. It was a desire that went beyond my mental mind; it was something that only my soul could understand, and only my soul could know what must be done.

Such was my longing that January morning. There are many who have this same longing. I, like others, had had this desire for a long time. Even upon reaching my teenage years I felt intuitively that someday I would be with a special woman—special in the sense of belonging only to each other. During college this desire to be with the right woman intensified. When I explained my frustration to my friends they suggested that I date every girl possible until I found one that I liked, but I knew inside that shopping for the right woman was not the answer. Later I realized that dating and living with a person on a daily basis are two different types of relationships. Because two people get along on a dating basis does not mean that their marriage would be successful. I thought to myself that there must be a better, higher way of attracting the right person. So I waited.

I moved to California from Utah in 1974, and I met a very beautiful girl soon after arriving. We seemed to be well-matched physically, mentally and even spiritually. I thought to myself that maybe she was the right woman at last; however when I would meditate and pray about her I felt deep inside that she was not the right one. At that time I could not emotionally face that reality, but when the relationship ended five months later I realized that, while our relationship had been right *for a time*, it was not the permanent relationship I was seeking.

Having become somewhat disappointed with my search I spent the next six months alone, associating only with a few close friends.

And then came that fateful day in January when it seemed that all of my years of frustration had come together and were staring me in the face. I pondered the possibilities open to me—I could either end it all or somehow find a way to release my burden, let it go. I recalled the words of a close friend who had found the right woman. This man had had many disappointing relationships until his pain and frustration led him to release his desire to God (or higher power). Within two months this friend had met the right woman. I reasoned that if it would work for my friend, maybe it would work for me. At least it was worth a try.

That night as I lay down to go to sleep I began to focus on all the frustration, pain and disappointment that I had felt about relationships. When I felt that I could bear no more I released or surrendered all of these feelings, pain and confusion and memories to God. And I told Him "Dear God, I want to be with the right woman, whoever she is. I do not care whether she is short and overweight or is 8'7", has blue and yellow polka dots on her skin, and has five arms. I simply want to be with the right woman, whoever she is." Race, creed, and color did not matter, nor did wealth and prestige. If she had eight children I would still accept and honor her, and her children. I knew that when I was with the woman God wanted me to be with, then I would be happy. And I also promised Him that I would accept the woman He brought to me. As I let go of my longing, along with all my frustration over this matter, I felt the entire burden of being with the right woman lift from my shoulders. The universe had heard my request and it had been accepted. I knew that it would be only a matter of time before I met her.

Sometimes when we ask for something from God and we are not quite ready to receive it, He prepares us to receive it. In other words, we are given experiences which help us to grow into our desires. About a month after I had released my longing to God I met a wonderful girl. She had previously lived on the East Coast and recently moved to California, and she was looking for a job. On the day that I met her she was sitting in an employment office, operated by a friend of mine, when I walked in. My friend introduced me to this woman, and we both felt a deep inner communication between us. As the relationship evolved, however, it became more of a friendship than a romantic relationship.

When we parted about a month later this brief relationship had been one of the deepest experiences of my life, even though there had been no physical or romantic involvement. At one point in our relationship when I confessed that I loved her she replied that she could not return my love because she was still in love with another man whom she hoped to marry someday. However, she realized she was taking a chance because his feelings for her did not imply marriage.

Naturally her feelings for me were somewhat guarded, but her refusal to accept my love led us to express our true feelings about each other. I remember one particular night that we discussed our feelings and our future together. When I left her that evening my emotions had been completely exhausted, and I could not even feel hurt or pain. When I look back at the experience it seemed to be a purifying or cleansing for me. To this day I still do not fully understand our relationship, but evidently it was something I needed to experience and clear out of the way before meeting the right woman.

Late that March, I was teaching a course with another instructor; she taught the evening session while I taught the morning class. Halfway through the course the other instructor decided to spend Easter with her mother in Southern

4

California and asked me to teach her evening classes. Earlier in the week I mentioned to a couple who attended both the evening and morning sessions that I always enjoyed students' comments because it took the pressure off me to say everything in class. The husband told me not to worry because Helga, a woman in the evening session, would provide me with all the comments I needed. So the next evening when I walked into the class I was looking forward to meeting Helga.

Helga did, indeed, offer many valuable comments, and as the evening wore on I felt myself becoming more and more attracted to her. It was not a physical attraction but something deep in my heart drawing me to her. She later told me she had felt something similar happening in her. When the class ended I knew I was attracted to her but I put it out of my mind because I did not think it was ethical for an instructor to become emotionally involved with one of the students.

The next evening the attraction continued to grow. I found myself saying things that were meant for her and not for the class. I thought to myself "Why am I saying these things that are not part of the class lecture?" Something inside Helga's heart was also telling her "I want to be with this man." At the end of the class that night Helga gave her business cards (she is a tennis pro) to the other class members, but she did not give one to me. I did not want to admit to myself that I felt deeply hurt when she failed to give me one of her cards. Again I thought to myself "Why am I feeling this? I hardly know this woman." Helga told me later that she thought it would be foolish to give me a card because she felt intuitively that we were going to see each other again. As we left the classroom Helga said that she did not feel like going home. Inside my heart I felt something building, like the excitement that builds when something spectacular is going to happen. I turned to Helga and suggested that we go next door to a restaurant and have something to drink. Feeling a bit apprehensive about the whole situation I asked the couple who had left with us if they would also like to go with us. Helga's eyes flashed anger telling me that this was between us and no one else. The couple, sensing the situation, politely refused the invitation.

When we arrived at the restaurant we had something to drink and again I felt that inner feeling that something was going to happen. After talking for an hour we left, and I offered to drive her to where her car was parked. The feeling inside had doubled, but I did not know what would happen. As I drove into the parking lot and stopped next to her car I tried to say goodbye but nothing came out. We sat there for a moment and I said "Well, I guess that's it" but nothing happened, we just sat there. Then she slid over by me and kissed me. It was not simply a kiss, but it came from deep in her heart. It said, "I love you, and I want to be with you." So we stayed there and talked for six hours. From talking to her I realized that even though she had been with many men, had been married once, she had never been truly loved as a woman and in her heart. And I guess I had never been truly loved in that special way either. And so began a beautiful relationship for which I am very grateful.

Three weeks before Helga and I met, she had a vision that I was coming. She was divorced with two children and had become discouraged over her prospects of finding a man who would truly love her as a woman and accept and love her children as well. I do believe in hope and in a God (universe, higher intelligence, or whatever you wish to call it) that answers our prayers. And as I look back upon our meeting and our life since then I am convinced of the higher power and its concern for our welfare, growth and happiness. Outwardly, it seems that certain events occurred to bring Helga and me together. I think that God used those circumstances to bring us together. What really mattered is that our hearts were open and both of us were willing to listen, and that has made all the difference between happiness and fulfillment, or discouragement and despair.

This is my true story, but it can also be yours. The pages that follow are given as a guide and message to those who are seeking that same fulfillment, peace and happiness that I have found in my life.

SEVEN QUESTIONS

Before we begin our discussion on how to find the right person, I would like you to answer seven questions. In answering them, be completely honest with yourself. How do you *feel* about these questions deep in your heart? Do not use quotes from other books or from friends but search your own heart for the answers that best express how *you* feel. It is all right to answer by saying "I don't know."

1. How does one go about finding the right person?
2. What do you consider to be the essential characteristics of a relationship?
3. What do you expect out of a relationship?
4. What are you looking for in a mate?
5. What is communication?
6. What is love?
7. What is the nature of sex?

Think deeply about each of these questions. Take your time. These questions are important because they will prepare you for an understanding of the book. Review them carefully.

By the end of the book you will have all these questions answered.

ONE

THE CONSCIOUS MIND
AND THE
WORLD OF INTUITION

*The boundaries of a man's mind are
set by himself, and no one else.*
ANONYMOUS

HAVE YOU EVER made decisions that turned out to be terrible mistakes? Most wrong decisions are made when people use only the conscious mind to make them. The true purpose of the conscious mind is to exercise free will in selecting our thoughts and determining their calibre. When we misuse the conscious mind by suppressing our spirituality, we are left with the logical or rational mind, the intellect, a mortal way of thinking. Remember how our school teachers taught us to make decisions? We were to gather all the information, sort out the facts, and arrive at a logical conclusion. Later on we were likely to find new facts which altered our previous conclusions or proved them to be false.

People who use the conscious mind to make all their decisions live in the world of regrets. How often we hear "If only I had known" or "Why didn't someone tell me this before, it would have changed everything." I remember stories in graduate school about frustrated Ph.D. candidates who, year after year, would learn new facts which altered their basic conclusions; as a result, they were never able to finish their dissertations.

Deductive logic provides a good example of the rational or mortal mind at work. This process involves a major premise, one or more minor premises, and a conclusion. This is called a *syllogism*. Here is an example:

Major premise:

All Italians have black hair.

Minor premise:

Mary is an Italian.

Conclusion:

Mary has black hair.

The same concept can be shown this way:

$$\frac{\begin{array}{ccc} A & = & B \\ B & = & C \end{array}}{\begin{array}{ccc} A & = & C \end{array}}$$

Looking closely at the argument, we find that it is perfectly logical, *but it is obviously not true* that "All Italians have black hair." If one of the premises is false then the conclusion will be false, no matter how logical the argument appears to be.

In college I took a course in deductive logic. After we had struggled through the semester our professor told us something startling, yet very profound. "Many of you will receive A's and B's in this class, but being logical doesn't mean that you are intelligent or wise." He continued, "Your arguments may be perfectly logical and your conclusions correct; however, if one of your premises is even partially false it will invalidate your conclusion." Naturally, the class became upset and asked why they had struggled to learn something that did not seem to be a very good way of thinking; students were aware that they used logic in their daily thinking and in making decisions. Our professor said, "So that you may learn a better way." We all wondered what that was. He said that using one's deep sense of intuition is a good way to avoid mistakes and make right decisions.

This intuitive level is often associated with the subconscious mind, but people often describe intuition in other terms such as "gut feelings" or "hunches." The intuitive level is just the opposite of the conscious level. When using our rational or logical mind, we find the facts first, and if they fit, we follow the conclusion. The intuitive realm is just the reverse. We must first follow our "hunch" and then come to know why.

Logical mind: why ————————➤ action
Intuitive mind: action ————————➤ why

Certain people already know the benefits of following their intuition. A few years ago in Spain two planes collided outside of Madrid; an incoming plane crashed into a plane that was taking off and all the passengers in both planes were killed. It was found that on the plane leaving Madrid all ninety seats had been sold, but only sixty people got on board. I'm sure some of the ticketholders didn't show up because they were detained in some way or found something better to do, but several people at the airport waiting to board changed their minds at the last moment.

One woman remarked that a terrible black feeling came over her. She felt intuitively that something bad was going to happen and she left the boarding area. A few others had similar feelings. Those who listened saved their lives. I wonder how many people had similar feelings but either ignored or rationalized them away. "What could possibly go wrong? The mechanics have checked the plane over. The control tower is carefully monitoring their radar screens, and, of course, the pilots have checked everything." Probably for a split second after the planes collided, they knew why, but by then it was too late.

The business world is full of these hunches or gut feelings, and fortunes are often made by this simple act of listening.

This example from the book, *Executive ESP*, is particularly interesting.

> Herbert Raiffe, owner of a Brooklyn toy factory, sounds the very model of an uncanny decision maker. In February 1972, President Nixon visited China and brought home two splendidly publicized panda bears. Predictably, demand for toy pandas soared. But Raiffe was ready. According to UPI, almost a year before, Raiffe had a "hunch." He felt bullish on black and white panda bears and ordered increased panda production at his factory to begin as of June 1971. It's hard to believe that in June, Raiffe clearly envisioned an American president touring the Forbidden City in the coming February, let alone that he saw the superfluous detail of Nixon gifted with pandas. Yet somehow Raiffe tuned in on a tide in the affairs of men—and toy buyers.[1]

The importance of following those hunches is summed up by another executive, Fletcher Byron, president of Kopper Company, who gave this advice.

> If you have a well-developed intuition, don't be afraid to use it . . . I have found that some of the most horrible mistakes we have made came after I ignored my intuition under the presence of what looked at the time like unshakable evidence.[2]

The conscious mind, when used separately, perceives a very small amount of knowledge that fits within its range of awareness. It is also limited by the five physical senses. In other words, the logical mind looks at what is around it, but it has no vision. If something isn't out there physically, it doesn't exist. The logical mind often holds onto doubts and fears. It is the world of *can't*, *if*, and *impossible*. I've heard people claim that something does not exist simply because they have not seen or experienced it.

We can easily see the difference between the intuitive and logical minds by following the history of inventions. Inventors have been described as functioning from this intuitive level, which is the level of creativity, new ideas, imagination, and true concentration. Rational-minded people sometimes call inventors quacks or dreamers. Yet many inventions that are commonplace today were considered impossible a hundred years ago. This editorial, for example, appeared in the *Los Angeles Herald Express* in 1846.

A man by the name of Joshua Coppersmith has been arrested for attempting to extort funds from ignorant and superstitious people. He claims to exhibit a device which he calls a "telephone" obviously intended to imitate the world of telegraph and win the confidence of those who know of the success of the latter instrument.

Well-informed people know that it is impossible to transmit the human voice over wires as is done with dots and dashes of the Morse code. And even if it were possible to do so, the thing would be of no practical value.

The authorities who apprehended the criminal are to be congratulated that it may serve as an example to other consciousless schemers who enrich themselves at the expense of their fellow creatures.[3]

The man who wrote this editorial saw only what existed physically at his point in time and space, which was the extent of his personal reality. To Joshua Coppersmith and others like him, reality includes everything the human mind can conceive. Coppersmith was not limited by his physical environment. In fact, he controlled his environment through the use of thought, bringing forth creative ideas from deep within his mind. Napoleon Hill has often said "What the mind can conceive and believe, it can achieve." If it were not for people of such great insight, courage, and creativity as Coppersmith, we might still be living in the Stone Age. True progress comes about as a result of inspiration from the Divine Mind.

Another invention, one of the most remarkable in the twentieth century, was first met with this response:

William Roentgen, inventor of the X-ray, was called dangerous and foolish because it was believed that his invisible rays would invade the privacy of the boudoir.[4]

Remember this one the next time you eat a salad:

Another quack said tomatoes could be eaten as food.[5]

Sometimes the rational mind and its logic borders on the absurd.

Charles Burton, inventor of the baby buggy, was called a fool by the public and his invention was outlawed as a traffic menace.[6]

In the past few years a new concept has emerged that is called *lateral thinking*.[7] When we try to solve a problem logically we sometimes seem to be caught in a whirlpool. Lateral thinking does the unexpected; it moves laterally out of the problem by using intuition. The best way I can describe it is to the use the phrase "coming out smelling like a rose" when all seems lost.

Edward Bono, in his book, *New Think*, demonstrates lateral thinking very effectively with this amusing fairy tale.

Many years ago when a person who owed money could be thrown into jail, a merchant in London had the misfortune to owe a huge sum to a moneylender. The moneylender, who was old and ugly, fancied the merchant's beautiful teenage daughter. He proposed a bargain. He said he would cancel the merchant's debt if he could have the girl instead.

Both the merchant and his daughter were horrified at the proposal. So the cunning moneylender proposed that they let Providence decide the matter. He told them that he would put a black pebble and a white pebble into an empty money-bag and then the girl would have to pick out one of the pebbles. If she chose the black pebble she would become his wife and her father's debt would be cancelled. But if she refused to pick out a pebble her father would be thrown into jail and she would starve.

Reluctantly the merchant agreed. They were standing on a pebble-strewn path in the merchant's garden as they talked and the moneylender stooped down to pick up the two pebbles. As he picked up the pebbles the girl, sharp-eyed with fright, noticed that he picked up two black pebbles and put them into the money-bag. He then asked the girl to pick out the pebble that was to decide her fate and that of her father.

Then the girl put her hand into the money-bag and drew out a pebble. Without looking at it she fumbled and let it fall to the path where it was immediately lost among the others.

"Oh, how clumsy of me," she said, "but never mind—if you look into the bag you will be able to tell which pebble I took by the colour of the one that is left.[8]

When I read this story a few years ago, I stopped at the point where they stood outside the banker's house and thought to myself "What would I have done in that situation? If I were the peasant I could have hit the banker and run for the hills, but then I would surely have been thrown in prison and my daughter left to starve. Or the daughter could have opened the pouch, seen the two black stones, and called the banker a fraud and a cheat. But that would only have made the banker angry and the peasant would still have owed the debt. But I realized that my logical solutions only came from my rational mind. The girl, on the other hand, used her intuition. She not only got her father's debt cancelled and saved herself from "a fate worse than death," but also allowed the banker to save face. I imagine the banker spent many sleepless nights wondering how she had managed to trick him.

Sometimes the intuitive and logical levels come into conflict. The rational mind will tend to ignore or explain away what the intuition is trying to say. (We have already seen this in the earlier example of the plane crash.) Or it may force a standard of conduct which the intuition knows is not correct. For example, imagine a Victorian lady entertaining friends in her parlor:

> The rational mind may be striving for social correctness: the Victorian lady arching her back in just-so elegance, while her intuitive level is making a running commentary about the foolishness of bending her body to the cultural norm, while her physical self is groaning with fatigue. A simple conflict, yet unresolved.[9]

The conflict between the logical and intuitive realms is not limited to physical health, but to most areas of life, including relationships. Sometimes what we consciously want in a mate is opposed to what we really feel in our hearts. People often get trapped by certain fallacies in their beliefs when they use the rational mind to select a mate.

One of the most common fallacies is that similar interests are necessary to a good relationship. Marriage classes in college do a great disservice in this respect. We are advised to seek someone whose background, age, and interests are similar, with the logic that the more we have in common, the better the relationship. I know one woman who is an excellent golfer and swimmer. She "reasoned" that since swimming and golf were her favorite sports she should marry a man who was also an excellent golfer and swimmer. She went through relationship after relationship until it dawned on her that maybe her priorities were in the wrong place. When this woman was able to give up what she intellectually thought was right in a relationship and learned to trust her intuition she found the right man.

Another fallacy of the rational mind is that it helps to make a checklist of the things you want in a mate. Sometimes this sort of list is divided into two sections of good and bad points, and then one comes to a "logical" conclusion about whether or not to marry the person. Many of these mortal rational marriages end in divorce after several years. The common remark is "If I had only known what George was really like, I never would have married him." In other words, the woman based her decision to marry this man on the limited external knowledge of her rational mind. In counseling sessions, people with troubled marriages will often say "We are both intelligent people—why can't we figure this thing out?" They fail to perceive that a relationship is of the heart, not the brain.

TWO

THE SUBCONSCIOUS MIND: YOUR MAGICAL BIO-COMPUTER

The outer world or circumstance shapes itself to the inner world of thought, and both pleasant and unpleasant external conditions are factors which make for the ultimate good of the individual. As the reaper of his own harvest, man learns both by suffering and bliss.

JAMES ALLEN

WE HAVE ALREADY DISCUSSED the rational and intuitive levels of the mind and some of the conflicts that can arise between them. The intuitive is part of the subconscious mind, which is a gigantic processor of information, a bio-computer. This bio-computer is like a hall of records which contains all you've ever learned, thought, experienced, and felt.[1] These memories are recorded in the brain, which contains the physical counterpart of the subconscious.

Each brain cell acts as a recorder which tapes our lives on strips of cinemato-graphic film. These films are described as small microdots which attach themselves to the brain cell. When triggered by outside events, these tapes or films play back our past experiences. For example, a word about love or the smell of perfume may trigger the memory of a past relationship.[2]

What all this means is that to some extent we are programmed. During our lives we pick up positive and negative programs from our parents, friends, peers, and teachers. These programs are dropped into the subconscious mind, which then acts upon them. By the time some people reach adulthood they are simply robots, playing out roles imposed on them by others. We are often programmed with regard to whom we should marry, what career we will have, and even what will make us happy or sad. Sometimes people break free from this programming and change their lives. Perhaps this is the reason one hears occasionally of a successful business executive who quits his job and moves to a winter resort to open a ski shop.

The difference between what we are programmed to want and how this can affect our lives is illustrated in the following story. A few years ago I met a girl from the East Coast who had moved out to California. She felt the move was right but she could not find a job in her profession, special education. One day a friend and I sat down with her and discussed her situation. After chatting a bit, my friend asked her "What do you really want?" She replied, "I want to be a special-education teacher in Northern California, get married to my boy friend, and settle down." We talked some more and my friend asked again "What do you really want?" Again came the same reply. It sounded like a tape. We talked some more. My friend asked a third time, "Yes, but what do you really want?" She started to say the same thing and then stopped and said "I don't really want to be a special- education teacher." Unfortunately, she had let her parents decide what career was best for her. When she became honest with herself, she broke through the tape.

The subconscious mind acts upon what is put into it. Thus success produces success, or poverty produces poverty. It is the force behind the scenes.

19

The subconscious mind plays a very important part in the interior life, even though it remains behind the scenes. Just as a good play depends on the scene, the lighting, and all the rest, so too our interior life owes much of its character to the setting and lighting and background and atmosphere which are provided, without any deliberate action of our own, by our subconscious mind.[3]

Once the subconscious mind begins acting upon a thought which it has accepted, it will run its own course without any conscious direction. This is why is is so important that we watch what goes into our mind.

There are three principles, or laws, that govern the subconscious mind. They are:

1. What we give or send out we receive.
2. The subconscious does not know the difference between right and wrong; it acts upon what is placed in it.
3. The subconscious takes everything literally.

Rule number one is actually very simple. It says that what we program or allow into the subconscious mind is what will return to us. What we give out are the thoughts and feelings, like seeds, that we have planted in our minds.

The oak tree sleeps in the acorn, the giant sequoia tree sleeps in its tiny seed, the bird waits in the egg; and God waits for His unfoldment in man. You will always gravitate to that which you secretly most love. You will meet in life the exact reproduction of your own thoughts. There is no chance, coincidence, or accident in a world ruled by Divine Order. You will rise as high as your dominant aspiration, and you will descend to the lowest concept of yourself.[4]

These thought seeds and the subsequent harvest, called the law of the harvest, produce themselves in a most detailed manner. For example, a shoe salesman in rural Kansas had succeeded in an area where other salemen had failed even through his yearly earnings were only $5000. Delighted with his success, his company sent him to the more lucrative areas of Minneapolis where opportunity seemed unlimited. However, at the end of the next year he had made only $5000.[5] This man believed, or was programmed to believe, that he was worth only $5000 so that was all he attracted. Other people do not limit us; we limit ourselves by our erroneous beliefs. One objective of being on this earth is the widening of our horizons by learning to let go of programs that limit the accomplishment of our true desires and hopes.

Many times the problems that one experiences in adult life can be directly related to negative programs picked up during childhood, usually in the first five to ten years. During my college days I knew a man named Bill who had been going to school for ten years but still hadn't gotten his B.A. degree. The one class he needed to graduate, he failed eight times! For a while Bill thought God disliked him. Something always seemed to come up at the last minute to sabotage his class. Finally he took a mind development course in which he was able to erase many of his negative programs.

Later, through age regression under hypnosis, Bill found that he had been unwanted as a child. His parents, struggling financially, resented him as an extra financial burden. To his mind that meant rejection. While he was at a family reunion at the age of four, Bill's relatives ridiculed him for not being able to tie his shoelaces. His subconscious mind, which always functions as a child, thought "I tried to do something new but I got ridiculed for it, so I won't try anything new in the future." More rejection. A few years later his parents moved to a new farm with a large chicken coop. One night his father complained about all the noise the chickens were making. The next day Bill went out with his dog and between them they killed about one-third of the chickens. Bill emerged from the coop dragging a dead chicken by the neck and his dog followed with blood and feathers all over his muzzle. When his mother saw them, she lost control and spanked him. To his way of thinking he had tried to do something to help his parents and had gotten punished for it, so in the future he would not try new things because he might get punished for the effort.

In high school, Bill worked on his uncle's farm. His uncle was the type who told you to do something but did not tell you how. If you goofed up, then he would tell you how dumb you were. One day Bill was hauling a hayload along a two-lane highway. As he went up a hill the tractor stalled. When he let out the clutch, the tractor rolled back causing the hayload to jackknife across the highway. After some thought he went back to the farm for another tractor and hauled the whole thing off the road. When his uncle heard about it, he told Bill he was so dumb that he was lucky to be alive.

When Bill left the parental nest and went away to college all these programs began to replay, and thus began his ten years of frustration. These patterns of rejection would create or attract situations where Bill would somehow fail the one course he needed to graduate. Thus Bill would fill that program which said he had to fail. (Often negative programs go unnoticed until the person leaves home; then they begin to take over.) Through studying awareness, Bill was able to erase most of his failure and rejection programs at last. He now has a B.A. in history, an associate degree in ancient languages, and an M.S. in accounting. The point to remember is that negative programs can be erased and positive ones put in their place.

The concept of "sending out and receiving" is especially true in relationships. I once talked to a young woman who mentioned that everyone she went out with began to fight with her. She could not understand why she attracted men with whom she would fight. I asked her "Did your parents fight?" and she said yes. As a child she had not yet developed her reasoning faculty (conscious mind), so when she saw her parents fighting she thought (subconscious mind) that fighting is the normal way of relating to your mate. This young woman was not an aggressive type person but she simply had within her subconscious mind a pattern or program which believed that the normal relationship between a man and a woman was to fight. Her mind, in this case the program, would create situations in which she ended up fighting with the men she dated. When this woman realized what had caused the problem in her relationships, she let go of her parental programming and her relationships improved; her awareness of the negative program took away its power and influence over her life.

One of the most common programs found in relationships is marrying someone exactly like one of your parents. A woman tends to marry a man like her father, and a man tends to marry a woman like his mother. What is amazing about this program is that the child's marriage can become almost a re-run of the parents' marriage. This story actually happened to two sisters, each of whom had married a man like their father. And they, like their mother, were very talented. She was a dress designer, an interior decorator, a hair stylist, a health-food fanatic, and a pianist. However, their father was what psychologists would call nonmotivated. He liked to sit in front of the TV set all day on Sunday watching football in a T-shirt with a can of beer in his hand. He also had a program which said he wasn't supposed to finish anything. One day he decided to expand the living room by knocking down the dining room wall. After tearing it down, he just left it. The girls' mother had to clean up the rubble. After twelve years of frustration, she got a divorce. The amazing thing about these girls is that they had situations exactly like their mother had. They summed up their conversation by saying, "Yup, just like Mom."

A young man, Jim, had lived with a woman named Mary for more than four years. He was a lead guitarist and had his own band; she had used him to build her own singing career.

When she finally became successful, she broke up the relationship. Then she decided she loved him and wanted him back. This time Jim felt it wasn't right and broke it up. Feeling that he had made a mistake, he asked her to take him back. She refused. After that see-saw relationship ended, Jim had four other relationships in a six-month period. The strange thing is that all of these girls were named Mary and all were singers who wanted to use him to advance their own careers. When he came to my workshop, Jim wanted to erase the pattern that had emerged after the first Mary, and he needed to let go of the emotional pain in his heart that had resulted from his experience.

This type of pattern usually appears when strong emotions or trauma are involved. It can occur in any area of life. One man noted that as a small child he had almost drowned. The terror of the experience was stored deep in his subconscious mind and in adult life, whenever he got near water his trauma from almost drowning would reactivate; the water triggered his memory of that experience. Even though he could not consciously remember what happened, he still felt the emotion that was stored in his mind.

We have seen from the above examples that "sending out and receiving" is an exacting law. Ralph Waldo Emerson explained the profound nature of this law.

The world looks like a multiplication-table or a mathematical equation, which, turn it how you will, balances itself . . . You cannot do wrong without suffering wrong . . . A man cannot speak but he judges himself . . . Every secret is told, every wrong redressed, in silence and certainty . . . The thief steals from himself. The swindler swindles himself . . . Men suffer all their life long, under the foolish superstition that they can be cheated. But it is . . . impossible for a man to be cheated by anyone but himself . . . What will you have? quoth God; pay for it and take it . . . Thou shalt be paid exactly for what thou hast done, no more no less.[6]

James Allen, in *As a Man Thinketh*, expresses it this way:

Every thought-seed sown or allowed to fall into the mind, and to take root there, produces its own, blossoming sooner or later into act, and bearing its own fruitage of opportunity and circumstance.[7]

From our previous discussion of sending out and receiving we also find the application of the second law: that the subconscious does not know the difference beween right and wrong, but simply acts upon what is put into it. It does not discriminate between what is right and wrong for you, but reproduces what drops into its realm through repetition, suggestion, and example. If the subconscious could make distinctions we would have far fewer problems than we now have. However, through proper training, the conscious mind can serve us adequately as the watchman to the door of the subconscious; it can learn to choose correctly what thoughts are allowed to pass into the subconscious. This is why it is true that if you "think only the most beautiful things possible" you will become those things.

Dream lofty dreams, acquire ideals, and realize and know that you go where your vision is. Cherish the vision of what you want to be, and cease complaining, and groaning about bad and good luck. Nourish that ideal of yours, feel the music that stirs in your heart, and contemplate the indescribable beauty of God and Nature and the loveliness that drapes your purest thoughts, for out of these frequent habitations of your mind will grow delightful conditions and experiences. Your vision is a definite promise of what one day you shall be; your ideal is the prophecy of what you shall at last unveil.[8]

If we harbor doubts and fears they eventually drop into the subconscious, which automatically carries out the orders given to it by the conscious mind. Then our lives begin to manifest the results of this negative thinking through misfortune, sadness, failure, hopelessness, and ill health. There is a very simple phrase to control and neutralize this negative thinking. Whenever you think something negative, simply say "Cancel, cancel." It works.

Sometimes people get caught up in playing certain games in relationships. One such a game is "The Savior." In this subconscious pattern, the Savior will attract a person who seems to need rescuing. The more the Savior tries to help the mate, the worse the situation gets. A twenty-two year old woman who had been through two marriages was typical of this pattern. She first married a drug addict. The more she tried to get him off drugs, the more he took, and she finally gave up. The second time she married an alcoholic. The same thing happened. After two divorces she knew she was doing something wrong. When she attended my workshop she had found the right man, but complained that sometimes he was so good to her that life became boring. After the workshop experience, she realized what she had, went home and got engaged.

Some people with low self-esteem have a program that says they can't stand to have it good, because this conflicts with their poor self-image. Sometimes these people, without consciously realizing it, will even try to destroy a good relationship. One woman who had met the right man told the workshop participants that she had such a program and had tried to ruin her relationship. But it wouldn't break, she said, because there was a deep bond of love between her and her husband.

An especially popular game among women is "The Good Provider." One woman came to the workshop who had been through three marriages. As she was from a traditional family in Arabia, her parents had arranged her first marriage, to an Englishman. It lasted eight years and during that time she had four children, but she had never been kissed by her husband! She said that her parents never allowed her to date and, unfortunately, did not tell her about affection and sex. With four children to feed and care for, she thought she needed a second husband who would be a Good Provider, so she married one—but that is all she got. The second marriage lasted fifteen years. Finally she couldn't take it anymore. She got divorced and married again, but to another Good Provider. He made plenty of money, but none of his emotions went below his neck. When this became apparent she began drinking heavily. Her husband, instead of helping her to stop, would simply keep her glass filled.

When her third marriage ended, this woman realized that somehow she was attracting the wrong men. Through the workshop she realized that if she wanted a lasting and happy relationship she would have to give up her programs about financial security, which we will discuss later.

A common game among men is "The Mother." Not being emotionally mature, they marry a woman to take care of them, to be a housekeeper or mother. One woman in this situation found her husband calling her "Mama" and her two little girls calling her by her first name! The reverse can also be true, that a woman will marry someone to be her father.

A man may marry a woman, not to be his wife and companion, but as a possession or object. Just as one picks out a new car or house, so these men (and sometimes women) select a mate as an object that they can show off or admire.

Other games are "The Hurt Little Boy (or Girl)," "The Victim," and "The Martyr." I think all of us have seen examples of these. The point is to become aware of such games and to stop playing them.

In these relationships where people are playing out programmed roles, the result is not two human beings communicating with each other from their hearts, but two negative programs supporting one another.

The third law of the mind is that the subconscious mind takes everything literally; it does not joke. The words and phrases we use affect our well-being. The subconscious mind responds to suggestions, not to reason. A woman found she had had several major operations in eight years because of her negative sayings. For two years she went around saying "So-and-so just galls me to death." The subconscious finally accepted the idea and she had trouble with her gall bladder. Another phrase she used was "So- and-so _____ me off." Six months later she got a urinary tract infection. Alice Steadman, author of *Who's the Matter with Me*, says that one of her friends went around for a time saying "So-and-so burns me up."[9] Her friend developed a fever, though her doctor could find nothing wrong. She had simply programmed nerself into a fever. Phrases such as "I don't care," or "I don't feel, or see, or think" can be very detrimental. I've heard people say horrible things like "I'd rather die," or "I wish so-and-so were dead," without realizing the power of their words!

Every thought we think has an instant effect upon the body and upon our emotional state. People who dwell upon negative things will sooner or later suffer in body and mind. Eighty to ninety percent of all disease is psychosomatic in orgin. We are a reflection of our thoughts and those who dwell upon positive, uplifting thoughts become more alive and vibrant. To these people life is a joyful experience.

In the realm of thought we become what we dwell upon. This includes our physical, mental, and spiritual well-being. "A man is not what he thinks he is, but what he thinks" or "People do not attract what they want, but what they are."[10] For example, God is love, simply because He dwelt upon love so long that He became love. In college I knew a man who went around warning people about being tempted by the devil. In time he became a religious fanatic. He was emotionally cold, unfeeling, suspicious, and vengeful, and his eyes were like balls of cold steel. Since this man dwelt on the devil he became one. He literally became the thing he was fighting against. People who criticize or condemn others become the criticisms and judgments they level at others. For every thought we send out, we keep the master copy. And we become those thoughts.

Thoughts are things; they are seeds of promise, whether they be good or bad. We are responsible for them. No matter what we wear, what job we have, or what we say, our thoughts tell others who we really are. The only person we are deceiving is ourselves. To put it another way, we become what we gaze upon.

A study was once made on death among doctors and, amazingly, most of them died of the disease that was their speciality.[11] We actually *learn* how to have disease. Once the subconscious accepts an idea it acts upon it, whether it is information about a disease or good health. Emile Coué, the famous French physician, cured many people through the use of their minds. He would have his patients sit in a relaxed position and repeat the phrase "Every day in every way I am getting better and better." This was repeated twenty times, three times a day. Since the subconscious operates on the more dominant of two ideas, Coué's affirmation bombarded the mind with a positive thought, which through continued repetition became dominant over the negative pattern and erased it.[12] This is the theory behind affirmation.

Children are easily programmed into failure with phrases such as "You never do anything right," "You are stupid," or "You'll never amount to anything." Coué recommended that parents use the words *success* and *happiness* around their children and avoid the use of negatives.[13]

A woman in Phoenix, Arizona, never mentioned the word "disease" around her children when they were growing up. She raised them in a cold-weather environment and they never got sick until they went to school. There they heard phrases like "You had better wrap up, or you'll catch your death of cold." When sickness was finally suggested to them and their minds accepted it, then colds, headaches, and flu became a reality.

People watching medical programs on TV often show up

at their doctor's office the following week with the same symptoms as those dramatized on the show. These people identify with the patient on a sympathetic level instead of a loving level. Sympathy only reinforces the negative condition, while love seeks to correct it. For example, a person who is sympathetic with a friend who has a headache may end up with a headache himself, whereas the person who is loving will look for a way to help get rid of the friend's headache.

Another concept to be aware of is the law of reversed effect. When you tell a child "Don't slam the door," what mental picture does he get? A slamming door. Another well-worn phrase is "Don't spill the milk." What happens? The child's subconscious gets the picture and spills the milk. Other negative sayings are "Don't get sick," "Don't catch a cold," or "Don't be late." To reverse these and to put them in a positive frame, we can say "Close the door quietly," "Be careful with your milk," "Please come on time," or "You are getting better." A lot of people say "Don't forget it" or "I forgot it," which can actually cause a loss of memory. The mind has an automatic scanner which seeks out the information you need. When we say the negative phrase "I forgot," our mind shuts off obediently. Instead, say "I'll remember it in a moment" or "Remember such and such" when speaking to another person.

Each word and phrase we use carries its own tone and vibration. For example, when we say the word *hate* every cell in our bodies tightens up. Conversely, saying the word *love* actually builds and strengthens one's mind and body.

A few years ago when I was living in Utah I went around for about six months saying "I hope a Utah driver doesn't run into me." Utah's drivers have a reputation for being careless. I gave no thought to the phrase, just casually repeated it three or four times a week. One day I was parked at a friend's house and a Utah driver in a high camper backed out of his driveway without looking and smashed my left car door. A week after I had my car fixed another Utah driver ran into the same side of my car near the rear fender. When I talked to my brother about what had happened, he said, "Well, you programmed it." I then said "Cancel, cancel," and that took care of that matter. The accident was not a co-incidence, but something I had programmed my mind to carry out.

On a more humorous note, a few years ago I attended the instructor's course for Silva Mind Control in Laredo, Texas. I met a man from Montreal who said, every time we left a restaurant, "Got no luck with the food today!" One day after class we went to a franchise pancake house for dinner. After we had eaten, our friend thought he'd like the house's special dessert, strawberry cream pie. As he finished giving his order to the waitress, he said "And make sure that there is more than one strawberry on the pie." We all laughed and he assured us that it was a valid hunch. When his order came there were one-and-a-half strawberries on his pie. When we left he said, "Got no luck with the food today." You can see how he reinforced this negative program each time we ate out. Several days later we went into Nuevo Laredo for dinner. Of all the things to order in a border-town restaurant, he asked for beef shish kebob; it was hardly surprising that our friend got liver on his skewer. Evidently the cook had put leftovers on the skewer instead of giving them to the cat. When we left, our ill-fed friend said "Got no luck with the food today." A few days before we left Laredo we went to the local lunch stand for a quick meal. He ordered corn dogs and I ordered two hamburgers. My order came and I ate my lunch. After about a half an hour of waiting my friend went to the counter and asked "Where are my corn dogs?" The waitress replied, "We can't find them." He left the restaurant vowing "I am never going to eat in a restaurant again."

Other people's thoughts can also affect our well-being. A

coach in a local high school mentioned that she and her staff disliked one of the coaches because he always seemed to be too happy. One day they got together and decided that every hour of the day one of the coaches would go up to this man and tell him "You don't look so well. Why don't you go home?" At each hour, beginning at 9 A.M., one of the coaches told him this and at 2 P.M. he went home sick.

How do we eliminate negative programming from our lives? First, we can begin using the words "Cancel, cancel," as suggested before. Another way is to understand thoroughly the nature of a negative program. Since negative programs are like tapes, we can feel the button being pushed in, the tape clicking into place, and away we go. When the tape is beginning we can shut it off before it goes too far, but once it gets going it plays to the end. When a tape starts to play say "You do not belong to me. You have no part of me. Go away."

Negative programs are like demons; they want to stay with us. They will even provide logical reasons why they should exist. For example, someone with a failure program may think of all sorts of logical reasons why he is failing. He may blame all sorts of outside conditions for his failure. When we admit our programs and accept them, then we can do something to get rid of them. Since we are aware of them, they can have no power over us. Once awareness comes, then we can shut them off when they begin to run us, and work to erase them. If we are not aware of the programs, we only feed them with our energy. When we deliberately shut off the energy, they have no support, and thus wither and die.

Several years ago a friend and I went to Utah for a visit. Since smoking is rather rare among Utah's Mormons, my friend thought the trip would be a good opportunity to quit smoking. Everything went fine until we got to Salt Lake City. One of my friends wanted a good dark draft beer and we found just the place, but this environment triggered my friend's program to smoke. He looked around nervously and started borrowing cigarettes from other customers. Later, back in California, he claimed that he wanted to continue smoking for a while so he could develop a stronger will to stop. That was his smoke program talking. It sought justification to support its own existence. When my friend realized this he refused to let the smoke program control him. Whenever he would feel the desire to smoke he said, "I am in control of my body and mind. I no longer need to smoke. Be gone." Within several weeks he successfully quit smoking.

THREE

MEDITATION: DOOR TO INNER WORLDS

Relaxation means releasing all concern and tension and letting the natural order of life flow through one's being.

DONALD CURTIS

T HROUGH MEDITATION we can easily enter the realm of the subconscious mind and influence it directly with the power of our thoughts. By using what we call *affirmations*, positive statements regarding our emotional and spiritual well-being, we can eliminate the negative programming from our subconscious minds. Furthermore, we go beyond or bypass the limitations of the mortal mind. We begin to tap that other 90 percent of our unused potential.

When we relax our personal tensions, we open our minds to the influx of a superior intelligence which tells us what we need to know and accomplishes through us what needs to be done. This great reservoir of wisdom and inspiration is the universal mind of God, of which our individual minds are a part. Each one of us can think with this greater mind when we relax our personal minds, clear the channel, and let the power flow through.[1]

And again

> When one turns his attention inward, he discovers a world of "inner space" which is as vast and as "real" as the external, physical world.[2]

Being able to function at this meditative (or alpha) level, we can expand our creativity, our latent talents, our awareness and intuition, and our learning and healing abilities. The inventors mentioned in Chapter 1 used these deeper levels to bring forth their ideas. These people were no different from you and me, except that they were able to tap that inner world. In other words, they simply used more of their minds. All of us can learn to do this. I think most of us have had experiences where we received information other than that from the five physical senses or the intellect. We often describe these experiences as moments of inspiration. At deeper levels of the mind there are literally no limits except those that we impose upon ourselves. By letting go of these limitations we expand into the spiritual beings we were truly meant to be.

Through these deeper mind levels we tap a universal storehouse of knowledge which can help us achieve our goals in life. A well-known writer in Los Angeles had contracted to finish a book for a publisher by a certain date, but he had trouble, and as the deadline approached he became tense and upset. Finally, desperate and exhausted, he threw himself upon his sofa, ready to give up his project.

> Then he fell into a deep sleep and dreamed that the top of his head was a giant funnel, into which were pouring all of the thoughts and ideas that ever existed. It seemed to him that a great ocean of intelligence was flowing down into this funnel. Suddenly this intelligence started to take the form of a story. It unfolded from beginning to end in the dream—clear, concise, and well- construc-

ted. Awakening refreshed, my friend resumed his work on the book and followed through to its completion, setting down exactly what had come to him in the dream.[3]

When this man bypassed his conscious mind by giving up control, relaxing, and letting go of the problem, his subconscious mind was able to reach out into the universe and gather the necessary information.

The physical body also benefits tremendously from meditation, which relieves the tension and stress that can literally choke off the body and destroy it. Stress is often called the unnamed disease;[4] some scientists feel that 80 to 90 percent of all disease is stress-related. At these deeper levels of the mind, the body is able to restore and heal itself. It is estimated that during meditation the body puts out ten times more energy than any at any other level of the mind. For example, one lady, a diabetic, felt she could not take the workshop because she would have to climb some stairs in order to get to the classroom. I suggested that by functioning at the alpha level her body would gain the necessary strength to climb the stairs easily. Each day she came to class one could see the improvement in her health, and she had no problem climbing the stairs. A few days after the class her husband told me that he had seen the daily improvement in his wife's health. He asked when I was going to start my next class. When one learns to relax and let go, the body returns to a more perfect state of harmony and peace.

For those who have never meditated, we can say that this meditative level is a state that exists between falling asleep and being wide awake. It can be those relaxed moments just before drifting into sleep. By learning to meditate properly we can go into that state and use it any time we desire.

Here is a meditation exercise which is a combination of various methods that I have learned over a period of several years. Our objective will be to relax the body and the mind; both need to be relaxed in order to meditate properly.

The Meditation[5]

Find a comfortable position and close your eyes. Experiment to see whether you feel more comfortable lying on the floor or a bed, or sitting in a chair. There is a tendency for people to fall asleep when they lie down. If you are tired and want to meditate on a problem, it might be better to sit in a chair; you might fall asleep if you lie down.

When you feel relaxed and calm take a deep breath and slowly exhale. Wait five seconds and say to yourself, *I am now at a deeper level of mind.* Repeat this same process two more times, slowly.

Throughout your meditation if you feel you need to be at a deeper level of mind just take a deep breath. This will help you to relax even more. When you become more experienced in the breathing you can inhale for the count of five, then exhale for the count of five.

Now count slowly to yourself from ten to one, telling yourself that at the count of one you will be at a deeper level of mind.　(Wait ten seconds.)

To help relax your body more, focus attention on your eyelids and relax them; feel them becoming heavy and feel all the tension draining out of them. Feel how relaxed your eyelids are. Then let the relaxation that you feel flow down through the rest of your body, down to your toes.　(Wait ten seconds.)

To relax your mind imagine that you are in a favorite place of relaxation. This helps the mind to be passive and to let go. You could imagine yourself on the top of a mountain enjoying the sky, your surroundings, and the peace that you feel there. Some people imagine themselves to be lying on the beach, feeling the warm rays of the sun or the ocean waves lapping against their body. One girl imagined riding her bike because she could feel the world go by and that helped her to relax and let go.　(Wait one minute.)

After one or two minutes of being in your favorite place of

relaxation, take a deep breath, exhale, and then repeat to yourself *I am now at a deeper level of mind.* (Wait five seconds.)

Learning how to relax our entire bodies from head to toes will help us let go of stress and tension and will put us at a deeper level of mind. To relax your entire body from head to toes focus on your scalp. (Wait five seconds.)

Now relax your scalp, letting go of all tension in that area and place it in a deeper state of mind. (Wait five seconds.)

Now focus your attention on your forehead. Relax your forehead. Let go of all tensions in that area. Now place your forehead in a deeper state of mind. (Wait five seconds.)

Follow the same procedure with the rest of your body:

Relax your brain. (Wait five seconds.)

Relax your eyes. (Wait five seconds.)

Relax the muscles of your face. (Wait five seconds.)

Relax your mouth and tongue. (Wait five seconds.)

Relax your throat. (Wait five seconds.)

Relax your shoulders and arms. (Wait five seconds.)

Relax your hands. (Wait five seconds.)

Relax your chest area—heart, lungs, etc. (Wait five seconds.)

Imagine and feel the tension and stress melt away from your heart area, and feel your heart working in perfect harmony and order. (Wait ten seconds.)

Relax your abdominal area. (Wait ten seconds.)

Now repeat to yourself, slowly and softly, but with meaning, *All the cells in my body are now working in perfect harmony.* (Wait five seconds.)

Relax your thighs. (Wait five seconds.)

Relax your knees. (Wait five seconds.)

Relax your calves. (Wait five seconds.)

Relax your ankles. (Wait five seconds.)

Relax your feet. (Wait five seconds.)

Repeat to yourself slowly, *I am now at a deeper level of mind, much deeper than before.*

Affirmations are positive phrases which we can use to recondition our subconscious minds while we are in a meditative state. Here are a few examples. Repeat each phrase slowly, quietly, and with feeling.

I now choose life.
(Wait five seconds.)
Every day in every way I am getting better and better.
(Wait five seconds.)
Divine intellegence now guides and directs me in all things.
(Wait five seconds.)
I now dwell only upon positive and uplifting thoughts.
(Wait five seconds.)
Negative thoughts and feelings have no influence over me.
(Wait five seconds.)
I now maintain a perfectly healthy body and mind.
(Wait five seconds.)

Now repeat mentally: *At this level of the mind all things of a physical nature are now balancing within me. (My cells, nerves, organs, and systems are now functioning in perfect order and harmony.)*
(Wait ten seconds.)
All things of a mental nature are now balancing within me. (My subconscious is now letting go of all negative thought patterns. It is now becoming a positive, helpful tool.)
(Wait ten seconds.)
All things of a spiritual nature are now balancing within me. (I am now achieving my true purpose in life. I am now learning to listen to the inner voice and letting it guide my life.)
(Wait ten seconds.)
I am now able to come to a total acceptance of all my experience. I now forgive myself and others.
(Wait ten seconds.)

Repeat three times: *I am one, one with myself. I am one with my surroundings. I am one with the earth. I am one with the solar system. I am one with the galaxy. I am one with the universe. I am love.*

(Wait ten seconds.)

To come out of the meditation, count to yourself from one to five. At the count of five, open your eyes, and say to yourself *Wide awake, feeling fine, and in perfect health.*

This meditation exercise should be used at first about three times a day—about fifteen minutes in the morning, in the afternoon, and before you go to sleep at night.

Meditation helps produce harmony in our lives. Thought precedes action. Thought is cause, and action is the result. (Every building had its conception in the mind of the builder.) Once we are able to realign our thinking, then we can realign our lives. In other words, an orderly and positive mind produces an orderly and positive life.

We become our thoughts.

FOUR

THE SUPER-
CONSCIOUS MIND:
THE HOLINESS WITHIN

> *The voice of the conscience is so deli-*
> *cate that it is easy to stifle it; but it is*
> *also so clear that it is impossible to*
> *mistake it.*
>
> MADAME DE STAEL

W E NOW COME TO the third portion of the mind, which is often called the superconscious mind. Other names for this level include the spark of divinity within each man, the Christ (or Buddha) within, or what Hindus call the *atman*. Perhaps the most common terms are the "voice of con-science" or "the still small voice." This aspect of conscious-ness to awareness as a voice, usually expresses itself as a feel-ing from deep within our hearts or souls.

Looking out into the universe, we may often wonder what keeps the universe going. Why doesn't one planet crash into another? What keeps the universe functioning in order and harmony?

There is an energy or essence that keeps the universe in order. It is the governing power of the universe, and without it there would be chaos. That same governing essence is found deep within each of us. It is our governing process.

Deep within us all there is an amazing inner sanctuary of the soul, a holy place, a Divine Center, speaking voice, to which we may continuously return. Eternity is at our hearts, pressing upon our time-torn lives, warming us with intimations of an astounding destiny, calling us home unto Itself. Yielding to these persuasions, gladly committing ourselves in body and soul, utterly and completely, to the Light Within, is the beginning of true life. It is a dynamic center, a creative Life that presses to birth within us. It is a Light Within which illumines the face of God and casts new shadows and new glories upon the face of men. It is a seed stirring to life if we do not choke it. It is the Shekinah of the soul, the Presence in the midst. Here is the Slumbering Christ, stirring to be awakened, to become the soul we clothe in earthly form and action. And He is within us all.[1]

This inner voice and power belongs to all men.

No man is so lowly but that at the touch of its secret this divine goodness may be brought to light in him. Even the animals exhibit its regulating and directive power. This goodness sleeps in the recesses of every mind and comes forth when least expected.[2]

This divine essence is in all things and gives life to all things. A chemist may create a blade of grass in his laboratory but he cannot give it life, which is a gift from God. This essence is Life itself.

The first step in understanding the superconscious mind, and how to reach it and use it, is learning to listen. During his presidency, Abraham Lincoln summed it up this way:

I desire to conduct the affairs of this administration that if at the end . . . I have lost every friend on earth, I shall at least have one friend, and that friend shall be deep down inside of me.[3]

This concept of listening is important. People who listen to the innermost level of their being usually have happy, smooth-working lives. People who ignore that inner voice often become lost or confused, and tend to have many problems. This is often reflected in their eyes, which are the windows to the soul. I'm sure all of us have seen people whose eyes sparkle with happiness and joy, while others who shut off that level appear to be faces without eyes.

When our thoughts and feelings are aligned to that soul level we feel happy and are at peace within ourselves; but when we disobey or reject that voice we feel remorse. For example, two boys may steal a bag of marbles; one may feel remorse afterwards for taking something that didn't belong to him, while the other boy may shut off that voice and let his ego think what a great thing he got away with. This remorse, which is a purifying process, brings with it a desire to do better and to live closer to one's soul. Remorse is not guilt, which is based upon fear. Guilt is used by individuals or groups to control others, and it separates people from God instead of bringing them closer.

Benjamin Franklin once remarked that "the best tranquilizer is a clear conscience."[4] In my counseling experience I have found this to be true. Most of the time, if a person tells what he or she really feels in the heart and then begins to use these feelings as a guide to living, the life usually straightens out. Often there is no real need to go through years of expensive psychoanalysis. Most problems arise when people are living a lie. Instead of facing what's deep inside they hide from it, focusing on all sorts of outside activities. When we are honest with ourselves and begin to listen, the solutions to our problems are already there waiting.

Everyone at my workshops who had been through a divorce admitted that they knew something was wrong before they got into the marriage. There were one or two exceptions, but in most cases the principle applied. Many times people would come up after class and say they should have listened long ago to their inner voice. I remember one woman from England who came to me during a lunch break and said "How true this has been for me." She had been married to a man for six years. Something inside had told her not to marry in the first place, but she went ahead anyway. She said those six years were like being in prison, and after the divorce she felt that she was finally free.

One of the most tragic examples concerns a man whose former wife kidnapped their ten-year-old son. When he married her he knew inside it was wrong, but he thought he could make it work. His wife turned out to be psychotic, and after ten stormy years of marriage they got a divorce. One day she took their son out to dinner and never returned. It had been over a year since they disappeared. When I talked to this man, he held his head in his hands and asked "Why has it taken me so long to learn to listen?" He was fifty-two at the time he said this.

Another girl found herself marrying a man like her father. Her heart said "No, it's not right" but she felt a compulsion in her subconscious mind to marry this man. She ignored the voice and followed the compulsion and was divorced a year later. She married a man exactly like her father.

One woman stood at the altar on her wedding day, knowing the marriage was wrong. After the marriage ceremony she knew it would never last. An interesting way to begin one's wedding night! How often does it happen?

A pathetic case occurred during my college days. One of my roommates—I'll call him Mark—had been dating a girl from South Africa for some time, and finally they decided to get married. Two weeks before the wedding Mark wanted to have a talk with another of our roommates, so they went out together and returned an hour later. I asked my roommate what happened and he said that Mark knew it was wrong to marry this girl but did not have the courage to back out. Shortly after the marriage Mark went into the Army. From time to time he would call us and ask if we were happy. What he meant was that *he* wasn't happy, but didn't want to admit it. Mark blamed his unhappiness on the Army (I'm sure that was part of it), but each night when he crawled into bed he had to live with the decision he had made.

Another aspect of the superconscious mind is motive. J. Allen Boone, author of *Kinship With All Life,* had the task of training a German Shepherd named Strongheart for work in the movies after the dog had had a career as a war hero. At first Boone had trouble communicating with the dog because of his ego. His attitude was "I (the great human) will train the lowly dog." No progress was made until Boone dropped his ego and began communicating with the dog as a friend, one heart to another. But instead of Boone training the dog, the dog trained him. The dog began sending him messages telepathically and teaching him about life. Boone also found that if communication was to continue with the dog it had to come from pure motives.

A most important and most embarrassing thing that my four-legged trainer drilled into me was this: No matter where I happen to be or what I am doing my mind is always much more on display than my physical body and the clothes I happen to be wearing. Neither my inner life nor his inner life nor the inner life of any other living thing is private or concealable. We are all mental nudists, always on public display for all freely to observe and evaluate.

The dog made me very watchful of my motives and very careful of the kind of thinking I diffused, especially when I was with him. And he made me do some genuine repair work on my character and conduct. There was no choice in the matter. I had to accept his personal discipline in order to keep our relationship balanced and functioning intelligently.

Practically every lesson that Strongheart taught me had to do with my mental attitude and its reaction on him, on us and on the various things we were doing or were unable to do. Accompanying each one of these lessons was the indirect but important reminder that he and almost all other animals, except those spoiled by human association, always live out from a pure heart, that is, from pure motives. He made it clear that if I wanted to get along with him or any other living thing, I must live out from a pure heart and from pure motives, too.

The more I tried to purify my thinking, my character, my purposes and my actions and to blend the best of me with the best of him in everything we did, the more the big dog and I began moving out beyond the restricting and unreal boundaries of our respective species. We found ourselves operating in the boundless realm of the mental and the spiritual, where each of us could function fully and freely as an individual state of consciousness and together as fellow states of mind in an adventure that seemed to have no frontiers whatsoever.[5]

People get into relationships for all sorts of reasons. A beautiful woman from a wealthy family in India married a successful American man who is communications chairman at a prominent university. After five years of marriage she had a big hollow space in her heart. She knew the marriage was wrong, and that she was living with a stranger. Whenever she approached her husband to talk about their problems, he refused to talk. The woman realized that her husband had married her as a showpiece, an object to enhance his prestige. Their friends were surprised to find out about their break-up, because on the surface it appeared to be such a good relationship. Her husband was charming, good-looking, and well-dressed, but all this was just a facade for his inner emptiness.

I knew one man who got married because he thought it would help his business. It lasted six weeks.

Often young people marry the most popular students in the class, the best looking ones, or the ones who have the nicest cars or the most money. Five or ten years later they find out that a marriage is more than material things. I think that is only one of the reasons why there are so many divorces among people who are thirty to forty years of age.

People often misinterpret success. I know a professor at San Francisco State College who teaches business communication. One day he asked his students to define their life goals, and 90 percent said that they wanted to make a lot of money, buy a nice house in the suburbs and get married. Success is not necessarily making it financially. Many people have come to my meditation courses who regret their choice of careers. They chose their fields for the wrong motives; often they had sought a field which offered a lot of money, forgetting about what was right for them inside.

There is nothing wrong with money when it comes as a result of finding your true career, but when money becomes one's sole motivation in life, life becomes empty and distasteful.

In one of my workshops, a man told me about a friend who had returned to college to finish his Ph.D. in education. The friend found, however, that the more he got into his courses, the more conflict and uneasiness he felt. Finally he quit and went back to being a house painter. His life straightened out and he felt contented and happy inside. In other words, his job as a house painter was right for him.

Jess Lair, author of *I'm Not Much, Baby, But I'm All I've Got*, said "What controls you is your God." People can be run by all sorts of things, such as fear, greed, parental programming, bitterness, hate, social prestige, and revenge. But it is the courageous person who can forgive easily, be honest in all his actions and thoughts, and be governed by the pure essence of love.

The voice of the superconscious mind is centered in the heart area. Just as the physical heart provides blood (life) to the body, so on a spiritual level the heart becomes the center of our being, providing us with guidance and comfort for our life's endeavors. The more we listen and trust that heart center the more light and love it generates, thus bringing an ever-increasing amount of joy and happiness into our lives. However, the reverse can also be true. The more we shut off that flow of love, the more unhappiness we experience in our lives. A person without hope is a person who has lost contact with the soul. When this happens, sadness, discouragement and confusion begin to take over life.

This can happen in several ways. We may continually refuse to accept the soul's counsel and commit actions which are contrary to the soul's purpose and nature; we may refuse to let go of an emotional upset which weighs heavily upon the heart; we may allow negative emotions such as bitterness and hate to build a wall around our hearts; or we may even sell our souls for some earthly gain. When this occurs, the body and mind suffer immensely. Often the result is an unnatural strain upon the *physical* heart. (This may be one of the reasons people have heart trouble.)

It is always possible to rebuild your life. In most instances the soul is patiently waiting for your return. When contact is reestablished, hope is rekindled in the heart and dreams of promise and happiness, once forgotten, again renew life. All that is required is a willingness to change, to listen, and to be true.

To help understand this heart level better, let's reverse the way we perceive information. Most of us do our perceiving through the conscious mind first, then it filters into the subconscious mind, and finally some bits of information may slip into the superconscious. Why not reverse this order? Perceive things by the heart first, and let the heart enlighten our subconscious and conscious minds. True learning is not from without but from within. The following diagram may be helpful:

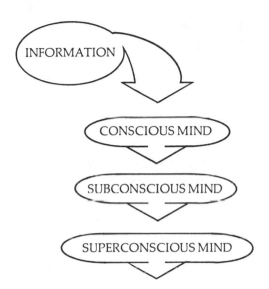

Now reverse this order:

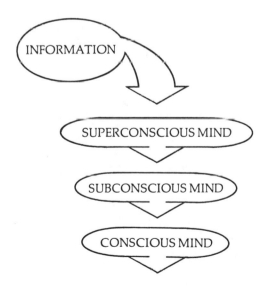

If this seems a bit difficult, try to imagine what your heart would say about a particular situation. You can ask yourself "How do I feel about this person or situation in my heart?" Or "What does my heart say about this deep down inside?" Does a particular situation cause you to feel uneasy or to have a gnawing feeling inside, or does it cause you to feel warm and content inside? In doing any of this it is absolutely essential to be honest. Being honest and truthful with oneself is important because it erases tapes that are not in accord with that divine heart center and gives the inner light a greater influence in our lives.

It can be helpful to talk to your superconscious as you would a true friend. Ask your superconscious to help you. Then listen. And always give thanks for the help given.

A woman in one of my relationship workshops was undecided about the man she was dating. She liked one thing or another about him, but she did not like some things at all. I interrupted her and asked "In your heart, do you want to be with him for the rest of your life?" She said no and her decision was made. It was that simple. Her problem was that she tended to fluctuate between her conscious and superconscious minds.

Sometimes people get caught between what they want and what is "right." My sweetheart once suggested to some friends that they attend a lecture I was giving on mind control. They had never been to anything like this, and wanted her to come with them. Since the lecture was on a Monday night she hesitated, because her favorite dance class met that same night. About an hour and a half before the lecture, I asked her "Have you decided what you're going to do?" She replied—"Not yet. I'll think about it later." "But you already know the answer, don't you?" I asked. "Tell me what it is." She balked for a moment, then said "I know it's right to go to the lecture, but I want to go to my dance class." She decided to go to the lecture, knowing that to be happy she must put the desires of her heart first.

By learning to listen to the heart and follow what it says, we begin to develop a trusting relationship with the God within us. When this contact is established and honored, then the soul is able to step forth and be a constant guide and companion. For this to happen, you must be willing to let the soul direct your life. The soul will guide you in any difficult situations that you may encounter, it will comfort you in times of stress and heartbreak, and it will teach you all the things you need to know. Most important, the soul will help you accomplish your most sacred dreams, and bring harmony, peace, and perfection into your life.

This fulfillment and joy comes as one learns to know God's faintest whisper.

Being truly happy comes about when we live by our hearts, which are hooked up to the universe.

> Happiness is becoming perfectly attuned
> To the harmony of the universe.
> Each person is a song,
> And the universe, a symphony.
> For the symphony to play well,
> We must be in harmony with the universe,
> Nature, others—and most important,
> Ourselves.

This process is like a flower opening up to the sun. Once we begin to perceive our own hearts, then we can begin to perceive the hearts of others. As we look deeply into ourselves and others, we see the real person—not the outward things and the programs, but what is really there. It is loving the person and not the mistake. It is loving people for being themselves and not for how much money they make, or how they look, or what their social position may be. At this level, there is no condemnation, judging, or even blame, but only a compassion and a love that looks past the outward faults and weaknesses and wants what is best and right for that person.

51

I remember when I first became aware of some of the negative programming that had been consciously or un-consciously passed on to me by my parents. At first I was somewhat dismayed and even angry, but then I looked deeply within their souls from my soul and saw only the magnificent love they held for me and their hopes for my happiness. As I did so, all of the faults and weaknesses that had once irritated me simply melted away.

My further study about this superconscious level taught me that all these former programs were really blessings and opportunities in disguise, and that by overcoming them I grew not only in stature and wisdom but also came nearer to my life's goals.

Most of life's battles are fought inside ourselves, and our greatest periods of growth usually come during crises.

At the heart's level there are no excuses; there is only responsibility for our lives and our destinies. Charles Fillmore saw this responsibility as a door.

Man opens this door or closes it at his will. Some open it just a little crack and others not at all. Some open the door wide, and they manifest such rare powers that they are exalted, even deified, by those who have closed their own doors. This little inner door is a door of great promise; he who opens it wide finds on its inner side the kingdom of God. It is the way into the kingdom. It is the Christ Spirit speaking through those who have opened; "I am the door."[6]

Our hearts and souls are always the departing point for all thought, feeling and action.

FIVE

COMMUNICATION: THE ART OF BEING HONEST

Men build too many walls and not enough bridges.

SIR ISAAC NEWTON

To love is to approach each other center to center.

PIERRE TEILHARD DE CHARDIN

THINK FOR A MOMENT. How would you define communication? In one sense, communication is being open and receptive, being honest with oneself and with others· It means speaking, listening to, listening with, and feeling with one's heart and soul. Our world, or our universe, depends in part upon being honest with ourselves and those around us. When we are honest, then the superconscious mind is able to work through us.

Motive is very important in this type of communication. Do we speak to impress others? Do we try to sell people something they do not really need or want, or do we try to use them to our advantage, not caring what is best for them? If we feel uneasy around this person, do we think of a million things to say to keep the conversation going instead of being honest and truthful? Are we brilliant conversationalists in order to hide from the unhappiness inside? Or do people trigger our programs, thus revealing an uncontrolled mind?

Often the words we say reflect not only our thoughts but also the deepest feelings of our hearts and souls. Each word we say carries with it a certain feeling or vibration, which can be either destructive or uplifting. It is our choice.

> Kind words cost no more than unkind ones . . . and we may scatter the seeds of courtesy and kindliness around us at so little expense. If you would fall into any extreme let it be on the side of gentleness. The human mind is so constructed that it resists vigor and yields to softness.[1]

A very wise friend once said that you can always determine the character of a person by listening to the words he or she uses. It is not what adorns a person but what comes out of a person that tells what is in his or her heart. Social position, wealth, clothes, material possessions, and education do not matter as much as sincerity, honesty, and inner beauty. Some of the kindest and the most genuine people I've ever met have been people with very little education and a so-called lowly station in life, while some of the most confused have been people who were highly educated and held important positions in their community. What a person is on the outside is not so important as where that person's heart is. For example, what makes a good teacher, doctor, or auto mechanic is not training but where the heart is. The heart magnifies or enhances any honorable job or profession.

Before communicating with others on a heart or soul level we must at least be willing to be honest with ourselves. The key to true communication lies in not saying anything unless it is in agreement with the heart, or is born of pure motives. Socrates and Plato always sought to use only words that were given to them by the superconscious mind. If the words did not come immediately, they would wait a few moments until the right words did come. Christ spoke no word "save the Father (within) commanded it."[2] Usually when people make the transition from their heads to their hearts they are quiet for several weeks until the soul or heart begins to dominate their words and thoughts.

When you reach this point your words will be filled with love and they will go out to touch and heal all those around you. One author expressed it this way:

> He who speaks from the lips chatters. He who speaks from an empty mind adds confusion to discord. He who speaks from a full mind feeds the minds of men. He who speaks from his heart wins the confidence of mankind. But he who speaks from his soul heals the heartbreaks of a world and feeds the hungry, starving souls of men. He can dry the tears of anguish and pain. He can bring light, for he will carry light.[3]

People who find themselves in negative circumstances can mentally surround themselves with white light, which either rejects the negativity or converts it into positive energy. This is one way people can protect themselves from the negativity of others.

One day I was talking to a friend about being honest and coming from the heart, and he remarked that for a time in his life he frequented cocktail parties. After awhile the parties became very dull and boring. People would talk about the same old things while consuming tremendous amounts of alcohol. He decided to do something to shake people up. He would ask two questions. One was "What do you think about love?" The initial reaction was generally silence, and most of the time people refused to talk about it; they could talk about sex and affairs but not about love. His other question "How are you inside?" was met with the same response. Usually people just refused to answer the question.

This man came to realize that these cocktail parties were not times for sharing the feelings of one's heart, but an escape from life. As long as people could drink and talk about external things, they could hide from what was going on inside.

In being honest we do not have to be negative. Sometimes what people call being honest is only an excuse for transferring or "dumping" their problems and negativity on others. A close friend of mine once worked as a medical transcriber in a hospital, where she found the working conditions intolerable because the office staff would dump all their problems, frustrations and resentments on her. The women in this office were either divorced or unmarried and they deeply resented their condition. By complaining they only reinforced their problems. Being open, my friend absorbed their negativity. After coming home depressed night after night she finally quit her job.

Once a woman who asked for her money back after completing one of my workshops called me up to express some of her feelings. She told me I was irresponsible, I didn't know how to teach, and the class didn't do anything for her. I replied that I didn't think she was being entirely honest with herself or me. Finally, she admitted that she felt terrible inside and needed help, but she felt guilty because she had previously taken an awareness course which said it was not ethical to ask for help. Once she admitted and accepted her real need, she could then not only receive help but also help herself. Her accusations were only symptomatic of what was going on inside, not her true feelings.

In studying truly successful people, not just financial successes, I found that most of them had achieved the dream within their hearts. They learned to listen, and not give up or sell themselves for something less than what they wanted deep inside. They held to their dreams until they came true. I heard one man remark that he had a friend who was truly successful (he found the right woman and had a career which he enjoyed immensely); this man thought this to be remarkable, since he saw very few who really enjoyed their lives.

It does not have to be that way. If people will hold to their deepest desires and dreams and not get discouraged, the dreams have no choice except to come true. But you must listen and stay close to your heart in order for it to work.

Many of the people who have lost that inner quiet, or contact with the superconscious mind, lead lives of quiet desperation. Several years ago, I ran across a story about a psychic healer who, discovering his ability, decided to go into hospitals and heal the sick. When he tried this he was met with all sorts of resistance, not from hospital officials but from the patients. He discovered that subconsciously they wanted to be in the hospital; some even wanted to die. Through their own negative thinking they had programmed themselves with an illness. Probably these people had very frustrating job situations or disastrous marriages from which they needed an escape. These people had lost contact with the God within and had lost hope. Their real sickness had been the unwillingness to be honest with themselves and to listen. By not listening, they paid the price of a diseased body and perhaps an early death. The key is to be completely honest with yourself and where your life has gone and where you truly want it to go. Then progress can be made.

The biggest problem about looking at a problem is looking at it. When we finally find or face it, it becomes harmless and easy to solve. The solutions are there waiting.

Throughout our lives we build up shields or defenses which prevent us from being honest and feeling with our hearts and souls. These shields can be like a fortress around the heart. Most people have "hurt" shields, usually built during the growing-up years as a defense against being hurt. Many times they carry over into adulthood and are nurtured through a tragic experience such as a sad love affair or divorce. People often say "I've been hurt too many times, no more! I won't let anyone inside anymore." The only trouble with hurt shields is that they stop most good feelings but have never been known to stop pain or hurt. *Only love can do that.*

A woman named Alice, who is a very close friend, had gone with Ted for over three years. During that time, Alice helped him to open up. Together they had bought a failing business and turned it into a success, but one week their business was confronted with a series of crises which broke up their relationship. That was about two years ago. Now, whenever Ted is discouraged he will come over to see Alice. They can talk about business for hours, but usually she will ask him "How are you inside?" and Ted will start talking about business again. Alice interrupts him to ask "But how is Ted?" and he sits there in silence. He has nothing to say because his heart is closed up inside.

I know of one marriage where the man will not completely open himself to his wife for fear of being hurt—as he puts it, he wants to have one last bullet in his gun. A mate's being closed can drive a partner up the wall. We need to share each other's depth, courage, honesty, and even vulnerability to make the partnership flourish. In the next chapter we will talk about the law of transmutation, which takes any pain, heartbreak or failure and converts it into happiness, love and peace within. You will never have to fear pain again.

Most of us wear masks so people will accept us. Because many people have a low self-image, they feel others will reject them if they present an honest face. So they pretend to be something they are not. Some of the most common masks are:

The followers. These people have strong fears of rejection. They fail to assert themselves and to be honest for fear of getting hurt. So they do what is "in." That way there is no risk involved.

The comics. Kahlil Gibran spoke about these people who always joke to cover up the pain inside. It is difficult to get close to these people or to have a serious conversation with them because they turn everything into a joke.

The intellectuals. These people feel it is socially prestigious to be able to expound in a scholarly way on any subject. They pretend to be immensely pragmatic. They usually confine their thoughts to their brains to hide what is going on in their hearts.

Mr. Cool. Supposedly nothing can touch or affect these people inside; they are cool about everything. Often they have a good job and a nice car, are charming and good conversationalists. In some of these people no emotion goes below the neck. All their outer charms are designed to hide the insecurity inside.

The machos. These males emphasize "manly" activities, often sports, and are usually aggressive, brutal and insensitive. They consider sensitive communication a weakness. They are like an iron fist inside and are very sad people. All they allow themselves is their skis, sports car, and physical prowess.

The seducer. These people think that sexual conquest will make them a place in the world. Their lives revolve around sexually conquering others and they usually brag about these conquests. A person is indeed troubled if conquering another sexually is life's greatest ambition.

The salesmen. Perhaps this is why sales is such a tough business. One car salesman told me that in the morning he puts on his "sales coat" and at night he takes it off. It is difficult to live with ourselves when we play a role all day, or something that people really don't need. I know one woman who worked briefly for a temporary employment agency where her boss told her to get placements in companies by any means she could think of—even by lying. She quit her job and kept herself.

The self-pitier. These people like to wallow in their miseries or problems. They enjoy suffering. They are pessimists. These people usually have strong feelings of unworthiness and rejection.

These are only a few of the masks that people wear. I'm sure you can think of more.

Jess Lair, in *I'm Not Much, Baby, But I'm All I've Got*, expresses some excellent ideas about communication. He found in teaching psychology classes that course information really didn't help people. Lair gave his students the same exam at the beginning of the semester and at the end, and the results were the same. In looking for a way to communicate with his students, he decided to come from his heart. The students arranged their desks in a circle, and Lair would say something that was deep in his heart. Then others would follow, saying things that were deep in their hearts.[4] (In other words, they said things that were in their hearts, not their minds.) Usually people who are able to open and express what is in their hearts gain a knowledge, wisdom and understanding of life that is infinitely more valuable than the memorization of facts.

Compassion is another important facet of communication. It is *not* sympathy or pity for another person. When we are sympathetic we lock into the distress of another person, thus reinforcing it. Compassion goes from one heart to another in love and forgiveness, wanting the best for the other person. In other words, compassion looks at the hearts of others—no matter who they are, what they've done to you, or what they look like— and desires the right and best things for that person to make them truly happy.

With compassion comes a deepened awareness of others and of life around us. This awareness expresses itself in being able to perceive beyond the five physical sense, the thoughts, feelings, and the needs of another. It is intuitively knowing what to do at the right time and the right place. In a relationship it means that special touch or caress when needed, without having to ask for it; it provides the right words for a troubled heart; and it understands a person's thoughts and feelings and knows their words without their having to say anything.

A husband gave this example about awareness and communication.

> The other night we got into bed, and my wife was very nervous. You know, rolling and tossing. I don't know why, but I started rubbing her back, and soothing her. And then I just held her face to face. I put my arms around her, and we just stayed that way. And this seemed to comfort her quite a bit, and she quieted down and had a good night. You see, I felt this might do her good, and I tried it. Which I'm not sure I would have thought of six months or a year ago. In fact, I suspect a year ago I might have lain there for a while and then said, "Well, I'm going to have a cigarette," and gone to sleep on the couch.[5]

Tenderness is another virtue. Husbands, wives and children will cherish moments of kindness and love much more than they will some material gift. A woman will always remember the touch or kiss that says "I love you" more than a new dishwasher or couch. I know men who buy their wives gifts instead of opening up and sharing affection; then they cannot understand why their wives are so unhappy after all they've bought them.

The following story beautifully illustrates the concept of tenderness.

> My, we had fun together—best fathers-and-sons outing yet! Gymnastics, wrestling matches, hotdogs and orangeade, and a movie. The works!
>
> In the middle of the movie my four-year-old, Michael Sean, fell asleep in his seat. His older brother, Stephen (age 6), and I enjoyed the rest of the movie and then I put Sean in my arms, carried him out to the car, and laid him in the back seat. It was cold that night—very cold—so I took off my coat and gently arranged it over and around him.

On arriving home I quickly carried Sean in and tucked him into bed. After Stephen got ready, I lay down next to him to discuss the night out together.

"How'd you like it, Stephen?"

"Fine," he answered.

"Did you have fun?"

"Yes."

"What did you like most?"

"I don't know. The trampoline, I guess."

"That was quite a thing wasn't it—doing those somersaults and tricks in the air like that."

Not much response on his part. I found myself making conversation. I wondered why Stephen wouldn't open up more. He usually did when exciting things happened. I was a little disappointed. I sensed something was wrong; he was so quiet on the way home and while getting ready for bed.

Suddenly Stephen turned over on his left side, facing the wall. I wondered why and lifted myself up just enough to see his eyes were welling up with tears.

"What's wrong, honey? What is it?"

He turned back, and I could sense he was feeling some embarrassment for the tears and his quivering lips and chin.

"Daddy, if I were cold, would you put your coat around me too?"

Of all the events of that special night out together, the most important was a little act of kindness, a momentary, unconscious showing of love to his little brother.[6]

I think most people would agree that, upon looking over their lives, their most cherished memories have been moments of tenderness, kindness, honest affection and truthfulness.

We could say, then, that communication is experiencing life at its deepest and most sensitive level, in one's heart and soul.

SIX

LOVE:
THE MIRACLE WORKER

Love is lost in immensities; it comes in simple ways.

JOSEPH FORT NEWTON

Love can cure heartbreaks, misfortune, or tragedy. It is the eternal companion.

ANONYMOUS

WHAT IS LOVE? This sounds like a difficult question, doesn't it? Love is a word used to describe or excuse many things, but what is it? Think about it for a moment.

Most people who attempt to define love only describe what it does. It creates caring, forgiveness, compassion, happiness; it renews the body and mind; it has the ability to take a seeming tragedy and transform it into a brilliant triumph; and much, much more.

Divine love is an essence, a highly developed, delicate and sensitive energy (or, if you wish, a substance). It is not an emotion, but it uplifts and purifies the emotions. It is the key to all creation. It is the power of God within man, and is the governing and harmonizing essence of the universe.

Love is a balm that contains the power of healing and of renewing and of everlasting life within its effulgent essence. Love is

63

the great refiner and beautifier. Love is more! Love is the key to every door. It is the creative reality behind every righteous desire and every ardent hope. Love is the cohesive power of the universe as it binds together atoms and substance. It holds families together—the world and the entire universe. If love were withdrawn all things would fall apart and disintegrate. When a human being eliminates love from his life he too begins to fall apart. Love is not only eternal but it is the most desirable element to possess.[1]

Everything that love touches is transformed into beauty and perfection. It is the Living Water spoken of by Christ. "But whosoever drinks of the Water that I shall give him shall not thirst . . . [and] shall be in him a well of Water springing up into everlasting life."[2] Love can take the loneliness and frustrations in your life and change them into happiness, joy and true achievement. And it can reach the most desperate situation and convert it to peace and fulfillment.

Annie Sullivan, Helen Keller's first teacher, taught the little girl about the meaning and power of love. Miss Keller, in her autobiography, says:

I remember the morning that I first asked the meaning of the word, "love." This was before I knew many words. I had found a few early violets in the garden and brought them to my teacher. She tried to kiss me: but at that time I did not like to have any one kiss me except my mother. Miss Sullivan put her arm gently round me and spelled into my hand, "I love Helen."

"What is love?" I asked.

She drew me closer to her and said, "It is here," pointing to my heart whose beats I was conscious of for the first time. Her words puzzled me very much because I did not then understand anything unless I touched it.

I smelt the violets in her hand and asked, half in signs, a question which meant, "Is love the sweetness of flowers?"

"No," said my teacher.

Again I thought. The warm sun was shining on us.

"Is this not love?" I asked, pointing in the direction from which the heat came. "Is this not love?"

It seemed to me that there could be nothing more beautiful than the sun, whose warmth makes all things grow. But Miss Sullivan shook her head, and I was greatly puzzled and disappointed. I thought it strange that my teacher could not show me love.

A day or two afterward I was stringing beads of different sizes in symmetrical groups—two large beads, three small ones, and so on. I had made many mistakes, and Miss Sullivan had pointed them out again and again with gentle patience. Finally I noticed a very obvious error in the sequence and for an instant I concentrated my attention on the lesson and tried to think how I should have arranged the beads. Miss Sullivan touched my forehead and spelled with decided emphasis, "Think."

In a flash I knew that the word was the name of the process that was going on in my head. This was my first conscious perception of an abstract idea.

For a long time I was still—I was not thinking of the beads in my lap, but trying to find a meaning for "love" in the light of this new idea. The sun had been under a cloud all day, and there had been brief showers; but suddenly the sun broke forth in all its southern splendor.

Again I asked my teacher, "Is this not love?"

"Love is something like the clouds that were in the sky before the sun came out," she replied. Then in simpler words than these, which at the time I could not have understood, she explained: "You cannot touch the clouds, you know; but you feel the rain and know how glad the flowers and the thirsty earth are to have it after a hot day. You cannot touch love either; but you feel the sweetness that it puts into everything. Without love you would not be happy or want to play."[3]

Love is the breath of Life in all things, even down to the cells and atoms of our physical bodies. We are made of love and love is our destiny. Love is the power of creation; without it there could be no growth or existence.

The transforming power of love can touch and heal situations which are considered to be beyond mortal hope. Starr Daily, the author of *Release*, had been in and out of prison during most of his early life. During his final stay in prison he went through a spiritual transformation which so altered his life that he dedicated the remainder of his life to telling others about the power of love and how it can change people's lives. Early in his life he had met the power of love, but only years later did Starr realize what had really taken place.

On another occasion when I was on the dealer's side of the table, I was an unseeing witness to this transmuting power of love in action. I was robbing the safe in the home of a priest. He surprised me in the act. From a stairway above me I heard his unexpected voice: "What are you doing here, my child?"

I wheeled, my flashlight and gun on him. He was in a night robe and unarmed. "Stand where you are," I commanded sharply. "I've got you covered."

"I mean you no harm." His voice had a rare accent of kindliness and honour in it. Slowly he began descending the steps.

"Stop, or I'll drop you!" I commanded him. With superb assurance he came on, reached the bottom, and walked leisurely over to the light switch and pressed the button. Turning to me, then, he said: "Put your gun down, my child. I only want to talk with you a little while."

At two o'clock in the morning I accepted this priest's invitation, went with him into the kitchen, and joined him in a cold bite. I left his home without taking his money. He shook my hand and blessed me. I had no fear that when I was out of sight he would exercise what the world calls duty and call the police. To this day I am sure he never mentioned my nocturnal visit.

What was this strange power he possessed over me? He did this because his love was genuine, not the romantic, sentimental emotion that men call love; but that deep sense of compassionate being which was so eloquently expressed by the Master when He said "Neither do I condemn thee." Nothing less than love could have caused me to act in a manner diametrically opposite to my habitual character as a criminal.[4]

The love spoken of by Starr Daily is not imagined; it is real. It is the most powerful force in the universe. It is the most delicate and sensitive and gentle essence in all existence. It is perfection, it is happiness, and it is peace. Love eliminates all striving, fear, doubt, and insecurity. With love there is no reason to hate or fear.

Love is also the promise of dreams come true. Love has the power to bring any noble and honest desire into physical reality. Any hope which is right for that individual—if visualized, and surrounded with love, and given thanks for—will have no choice but to come true.

Love is intellegence. It is not necessary to control love or to tell it what to do. Our task is to send love out, and let it do its precious work. For love brings harmony and perfection into any situation it touches.

One young woman, who had one of those long (four-year) on-off romances, was distressed because her former boyfriend would not stay away. I suggested sending love to him and she thought "Won't that make him come back to me?" I said "If you resent him that will tie you to him, but if you send him love it will release him to find the right woman." She tried it and it worked.

We do not have to force love to do our bidding; it will automatically do the right thing.

When we look at people through the eyes of love there is no condemning or judging, only wanting the best for that person or situation. Love allows a person to grow and find his rightful place in his heart and on the earth.

Love is the key; love is the healer. It is not true, as some "authorities" claim, that love hurts or destroys. That kind of so-called love is only the emotional attachment to something in the subconscious mind, it is not love. Real love can clear the mind and help straighten out the messes in one's life, or it can heal and energize the body. It can heal all imagined or real hurts, and it can help one to become more sensitive and aware.

To know and experience God's love, one must learn to generate love. It is quite simple. Go to your meditative level as explained in Chapter 3 and, when you are relaxed, begin to imagine waves of love or light flowing out from your heart center (solar plexus), your mind, and your body.

Imagine these waves coming from your entire body. They

are coming off the top of your head, your forehead, your face, the back of your head, and your eyes.

Now imagine waves of love coming from your throat, your shoulders, arms, and hands. Now the waves of love are coming off your chest, lungs, heart, back, abdominal area, legs, knees, calves, ankles, and feet.

Now send this love out in waves to fill the room you are sitting in, then the town or city in which you live, then your region, your state, and finally the entire earth.

Now imagine these waves of love flowing from you throughout the solar system, throughout the galaxy, and throughout the universe to that Source of Light and Truth whence you came.

For variation, you could imagine these waves of love in colors of blue, gold, and rose. Or simply imagine a brilliant golden white light coming off of you.

If you have any bodily aches and pains, intensify the love through those areas. This is important. Usually people think that they should imagine love flowing into an afflicted area, but instead imagine the love flowing *from* that area.

I remember sharing this love experience with a woman who had a severe eye problem. When I mentioned generating love out of any afflicted area she began pouring love through her eyes; in other words, her eyes became generators of love. That same evening as she was driving home her eyes began changing focus. She became frightened and went to see her eye doctor the next day. After examining her eyes, her doctor told her in amazement that her right eye, the one most afflicted, was now perfectly healthy.

Another woman who had a blood clot in her lower leg began having the clot generate love, and the clot dissolved. Instead of being a source of pain and danger, that clot became a generator of love.

If you have any situation, person or problem which needs to be resolved or forgiven, simply surround it with love and let it go. Or, if someone needs your help, surround that person with love and bless and release them. Remember to let love do the work.

The key to making this exercise work is learning to generate love with all of the heart, mind and body. We unite all three of these levels in love with all our strength. Most people use their strength when they are angry, but we can reverse it and generate love.

It is beneficial to generate love for a few minutes when you get up in the morning and before falling asleep at night. Anytime during the day when you are offended or hurt, stand silent for a moment and generate love. If someone needs your help, generate love and sent it to them.

What we are actually doing is learning to use our hearts as love generators instead of knife holders or shock absorbers. Our hearts are now becoming powerful transforming centers to transform the negatives in our lives.

When we acknowledge that love is the first principle of existence, we realize that most problems in the world today are caused by a lack of love. It is startling to note that there are many who go through their entire lives without knowing or feeling true love.

Several years ago I began holding special workshops to help children learn how to generate love and dispel the negativity in their lives. During the love exercise I asked them when they felt love coming forth from their heart centers to raise their hands. About 60 percent did. The others, I imagine, didn't know what love was or did not know how to accept it. One small boy who remained downcast during the exercise was asked what was troubling him. He said nothing, but still would not look into our eyes. Several of us told him we wanted to be friends with him. Unsure of what to do in the situation, he pulled out a five-dollar bill that his parents had given him for the workshop. Since he probably had never felt or accepted love, he attempted to offer a substitute in its place.

For a child or any human being to fully mature emotionally and spiritually it is necessary to have love as a foundation. Love is the ultimate teacher and educator.

Learning to generate love can be very helpful in letting go of the guilt, frustration and pain that are experienced in relationships. Several years ago I had an old relationship program start to play and I couldn't seem to get rid of it. I went to see a friend, and when I walked in his door he noticed the dark cloud over my head. He said "It looks like you've really got a problem." I said yes. He added, "You really like those programs, don't you?" Again I answered yes. He had me sit down and generate love for about five minutes. When I opened my eyes the pain and confusion had disappeared. During the day they would try to sneak back, so I generated love each time. Since then I've never had any problem with that program.

A young man ended a relationship with a woman he had gone with for two years. It had been a beautiful relationship and when she left he tried hating her, but that made him feel terrible. Then he tried self-pity, but that didn't help either. Next he tried depression, and stopped all feeling. Finally, he recalled all of their beautiful experiences together, gave thanks for them and sent her love. Poof! She was gone.

Another man had trouble finishing one of my classes because he felt guilty about divorcing his wife. He knew they shouldn't be together, but she had no means of supporting herself. By his guilt he actually held on to her, preventing her success. He could not let her go. During one of the breaks he sat in a chair, focused on his former wife, and sent her all the love he had in his heart. A shudder ran through his body and she was gone. He later remarked that this had been one of the most profound experiences of his life.

One of the most beautiful examples of how love can erase old relationship programs happened to a woman in one of my classes. This woman broke up with her boyfriend on a Sunday and came to class the following Tuesday; her boyfriend showed up in the same class with his new friend. By

Thursday she couldn't take any more and began crying during one of the mental exercises. At the break I took her down the hall and asked if she could let go of her problem. She only cried louder. She didn't really love this man but all of the pain and anguish from her three previous marriages seemed to be staring her in the face. I sat down with her and she generated love for about ten minutes and the pain was gone. She went back into the class and was fine for the remainder of the course. The negative programs never again returned.

Whenever one seeks a deeper solution to any problem, love is always the answer. It always has been. In a sense this woman's story is a miracle because love has touched and transformed it. *Where there is love there is always a miracle.*

By letting go of these old relationship patterns we free ourselves from any future influence they might have. When we are controlled by the past through programs of pain, frustration or bitterness, then these programs constantly replay, and we continue to have relationships in which only pain and frustration are experienced. Generating love releases the past and turns it into love. Your past does not have to be your future; the slate can be wiped clean and you can begin life anew. *What we dwell upon now we become in our future. If love is what we dwell upon, then love becomes our future.* The accompanying diagram may help.

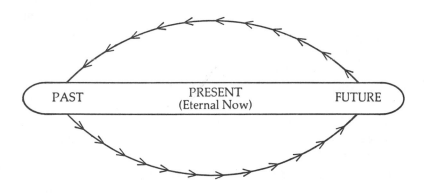

In the center of the diagram is written the word Present. When, through love, we let go of all our old programs we then live in the Present or Eternal Now, which is love. Our future is then filled with all the things that love can provide.

Many people make it a practice to generate love wherever they go or whatever they do.

I know an older woman who rides the bus to work every day in Oakland. During these trips she generates love to everyone on the bus. One day as she was generating love a young man got on the bus and walked toward the back, looking for a place to sit. He sat down next to her, though there were other empty seats on the bus. Then he put his arm around her. He sat there and said nothing. When he came to his stop he got off the bus, never saying a word.

Another time, as she sat in the back of the bus generating love, a man got in and sat next to her. After about fifteen minutes he got up to leave, turned to her and said "And God bless you, too."

Love can also harmonize our working conditions.

One woman spoke of her experience as a salesperson for a large distributing company. One of the managers of the five stores she supplied started a rumor that she was cheating on the accounts of her customers. At first she was very angry, but then she settled down and began to send love to the manager—lots of it. Two days later she received a call from a man who identified himself as the manager of one of the stores she serviced. He told her that, for some reason which he did not fully understand himself, he had started the rumor. He was deeply apologetic and assured the woman that he would call all the stores and tell them the story was a rumor and that he had spread it. She checked the other stores and sure enough, he called them all.

Another girl works in the complaint department of a large department store. At night she would often come home nervous and discouraged after being harrassed all day by irate

72

customers. Then she found out how love works and started generating it around the office and to all who came into it. When she saw an angry customer come in she would immediately send love to that person, and some of them began to smile and even forgot why they came in. Through love she had changed the atmosphere of her office from one of negativity to one of love and happiness for both herself and her customers.

Love also can erase the little resentments or grudges which people carry around for months and sometimes years. A year and a half ago, a tennis player in one of my classes was having trouble letting go of an old tennis match, an important semi-professional match during which her opponent had cheated and won. This woman had carried resentment toward that opponent for six months. During the class I mentioned that some people, when in a relaxed state of mind, put all their troubles in a box, wrap it up, and send it in a rocket ship to the moon. The woman decided to try this technique to help her let go of the grudge, but she said that when she had done it the rocket ship kept returning to earth. She just couldn't seem to let go of her grudge. One day I spoke about sending love to your enemies, those who use or persecute you, or dislike you. As I said this a smile came across her face and she said "She's gone."

Many of our old programs are based on fear. I have found that many people are motivated by one type of fear or another. Common fears include being hurt, growing old, losing a loved one, divorce, poverty, loneliness, pain, rejection, or failure. Love can enfold all of these fears and transmute them into light.

Love not only erases the negatives in us but also in all those who have suffered as a result of our mistakes. Children are a good example of this, as they are sometimes exposed to the least noble aspects of our personalities; many times the eldest child is the particular target. These conditions can be erased in our children as well as in ourselves. As we surround our old programs with love and let them go, they are also erased from our children's minds. This is also true for friends, parents, former lovers, wives or husbands.

Where there is love there is also forgiveness; as there can be no love without forgiveness; there can be no forgiveness without love. Just as love is the foundation upon which our universe operates, so is forgiveness. Being able to forgive includes looking past the physical and mental weaknesses into the heart of an individual, and letting go of any wrongs, real or imagined, that he or she may have done, then blessing that individual by truly desiring what is right and true for that individual. Through forgiveness the power of love is released in one's life. Forgiveness becomes easy when we love, and only becomes difficult when we let our emotions and intellects interfere.

Forgiveness contains the power to release us from the bondage of our doubts, fears, resentments and hates. Sometimes we resist letting go of our faults, but through the act of forgiveness they can be released. As we learn to forgive, the desire to hurt ourselves and others is lost.

When one's lips and mind have lost the power to hurt and wound, then one's Voice will be heard among the Gods.[5]

And as we forgive we are forgiven:

He that cannot forgive others breaks the bridge over which he himself must pass if he would ever reach heaven; for everyone has need to be forgiven.[6]

Nor can conditions be placed upon forgiveness ("If so-and-so will do this, then I will forgive her."). Forgiveness is not of the intellect but a natural act of the heart; love forgives without reasons.

Many problems of ill health have been helped simply by forgiving. If we are to keep our mental and physical health and our spiritual well-being, we must bring the power of forgiveness into our lives.

Sometimes it is difficult to love and forgive because of the pain and hurt we are suffering. This can be overcome by learning to generate love and to forgive instantly.

Forgiveness is an essential part of any relationship, old or new. Many divorcing people go around saying things like "After all I've done for you," "It's all your fault," "If you hadn't done such-and-such, this never would have happened," "I've given you the best years of my life," or "You've changed, why can't you be like you were when we first married?" Others go for years living lives of pain and misery in order to prove their former mate wrong. "I'm going to remain unhappy for the rest of my life to prove that you were wrong in divorcing me." In such instances, the real loser is the one who has forgotten to forgive. In these situations people often accuse each other of all sorts of things.

The word *devil* means *accuse*. Blame has no place in our heart or lives—it is just something the ego uses to prop itself up with. When we listen to the superconscious mind we find that many marriages did not feel right to begin with, so why should there be blame? Other relationships are right for a time and then end. They are part of our growing and maturing process, helping us find out who we are and what we want out of life. When a romantic relationship ends, look at it this way: Where there are two unhappy people, now there can be four happy people.

What we are actually doing is opening our hearts to love and giving up our pains, hatreds, failures, and heartbreaks. Some people have become so used to being bitter or hateful that they are afraid to love; they are so attached to their weaknesses that they love them more than God or what is right and good. When one is able to put love and forgiveness first then one can be truly free and happy.

Another way of bringing love into our lives is through the power of relinquishment. Relinquishment is surrendering or giving up the problem to God. Often pain and suffering will lead us to a point of spiritual awareness after all possible physical and mental solutions have been exhausted. The stress of the situation demands a solution beyond all mortal capabilities, and it is at this time that an individual will relinquish control over a problem and give it to God, asking that His will be done.

Margaret, an older woman, told this story. She had dated a married man for over five years, but he refused to marry her because every time he tried to divorce his wife she would threaten to commit suicide. The previous two years of their relationship had become very painful because it was apparent that the relationship would not progress any further. One night Margaret mentioned that the pain she was experiencing was becoming unbearable and she needed to resolve the situation. I suggested that she go home and pour out her heart to God and put the relationship in His hands. She went home that night and literally poured out her heart to God about the man she loved. She also forgave this man and released him to God. As she did so she felt waves of love flowing through her, erasing the pain and anguish in her heart. Later that week she ended the relationship and has been happier ever since.

During college I was rooming with a very close friend. That year his finances were low and I ended up paying the room rent, but after about eight months I became frustrated because he still wasn't paying rent. One day I asked him why he couldn't get some type of job, but he didn't say anything. I became angry and threw one of my shoes into the wall, damaging it. Later that day I looked at what I had done and realized that it was foolish to let something like finances interfere with the best friendship I had ever had, so I made a commitment to be a friend. If he wanted the rest of my savings I would give them to him gladly—whatever it took to be a real friend I would do. Two things happened from this experience. Our friendship grew even closer after that, probably because I was willing to put him first, and his financial problems were solved within two weeks. As I was willing to let go of the labels I had placed upon him and only desire his highest good, he was enabled to release and solve his problem.

At the heart level life is different, because we are functioning from a much deeper level then just the physical or mortal planes. Often people will shift between their conscious and superconscious minds. Once a woman who said she had never felt love before, wondered if sending out love would attract "weird" people to her. I asked her "What does your heart say about generating love?" She replied that it felt good and she should do it because it would change her life, but then she shifted back to her rational mind with all its doubts and limitations. I finally told her always to listen to that heart level and follow it. As she does, it will become stronger, and thus she will come to feel more secure about listening to her heart.

SEVEN

GRATITUDE:
THE SONG OF THE SOUL

And he who receives all things with thankfulness shall be made glorious; and the things of this earth added unto him.

DOCTRINE & COVENANTS 78:19

Rejoice evermore. Pray without ceasing. In everything give thanks: for this is the will of God in Jesus Christ concerning you.

I THESSALONIANS 5:16-18

DO YOU HAVE A PROBLEM, fear or worry that you haven't been able to solve? The solution is very simple. Give sincere and heartfelt thanks for the situation exactly as it is.

If anyone would tell you the shortest, surest way to all happiness and perfection, he must tell you to make it a rule to yourself to thank and praise God for everything that happens to you. For it is certain that whatever seeming calamity happens to you, if you thank and praise God for it, you will turn it into a blessing. [1]

There is an actual power in thanksgiving which is often called the *law of transmutation.* Love is the creative essence of the universe and gratitude or praise are the keys which increase the flow of love into one's life. When we adopt an attitude of being thankful in all things love is released in our lives.

But you may ask "How can I be thankful for negative conditions such as a tragedy, crisis or disaster?" Being thankful is the spiritual law of transmutation. Sometimes the law of gratitude is called spiritual alchemy, which means "all chemistry."[2] It is taking a negative condition and, through praise and gratitude, turning it into a blessing of love. There is an actual conversion process that takes place. When we give thanks for something negative and accept it as His will, the condition is lifted into God's hands and love flows into the situation. Praise, or gratitude, is love or faith in action.

Praise is the catalyst which changes a negative circumstance into a positive one. This process can be compared to the change that takes place when a photograph is developed or is converted from a negative into a print.

> When we hold a photo negative up to the light all objects are reversed: Black is white, white is black. Moreover, the character lines of any face in the picture are not clear. Once placed into the developing solution, what photographers call "the latent image" is revealed in the print—darkness is turned to light; and, lo, we have a beautiful picture.[3]

In this case, the developing solution or chemical is the gratitude we use to transmute our negative conditions.

Napoleon Hill saw this law of transmutation as the seed of equivalent benefit: "Within every disappointment, heartbreak, or failure, there exists an equal (usually greater) positive benefit."[4] Abraham Lincoln failed nine times in various careers before he arrived at the presidency; the point is that each failure was a blessing or an opportunity in disguise. Each so-called failure changed the course of his life enough to lead him into politics and eventually to become our nation's leader. There is a great difference between a man who has failed three times and one who says "I am a failure."

The seed of equivalent benefit also applies to relationships. People who have found the right person are thankful their previous relationships didn't work out as expected. Many times these previous relationships were growing experiences which were right for a time, but not an entire life. If a relationship hasn't worked out, it usually means there is a right person out there waiting for you. If we can take each disappointment and accept it, surround it with love, give thanks for it, and then release it, we can go forward to the fulfillment of our life's dreams.

After I met the right woman and we had been going together for several months, she decided that she preferred another man whom she had recently met. So we parted. The first thing I did was banish all ideas about getting back with her, as I found it too painful to even think about. I examined my feelings about her and looked deeply into my heart to see if we really belonged together or not. I felt the relationship was right, but my primary concern was to let her go emotionally and somehow transmute the heartache I was feeling. I had two paths open to me: I could close off the feelings of my heart and become bitter and hollow, or I could give thanks for our relationship and even for breaking up. I chose to do the latter. For the next few days my only thoughts were "Thank you, Father." I continually repeated it throughout the day and often into the night. Within three days I felt a strength and joy coming from within me that I had not felt before. The thankfulness was literally converting the pain into love.

My next step was to release her by praying for her happiness, with me or with someone else. In this way I could release her to God and allow His influence into our lives. If we returned to each other then I would be certain that it was right, but if she did not come back I knew that someone special would be given to me. In other words, I released her to God and asked that His will be done. Two weeks later we were back together again.

One young woman who had broken up with her boyfriend gave thanks for her situation in this way. Instead of closing up her heart she asked God to take the pain she felt inside and use it to help others in the same situation. As she did so, the pain disappeared and her heart opened up more than it ever did before. With this opening up she felt a deep compassion for all mankind and began praising God. This woman later remarked that she was somewhat startled by the experience because she had no previous knowledge that anything so deep and profound could happen to her or anyone.

Linda, a close friend, had married the right man but they ran into some negative programs in each other which threatened their relationship. One day she called me, distraught because her husband was planning to leave her. I told her no matter what happened to just give thanks for it. I didn't hear from her for several weeks and I wondered what had happened. One day I called her to ask how things were going and she said that she and her husband had worked through their programs and everything was fine now. She said that what helped her immensely during this time was giving thanks for the situation as it was. Thus, she was able to transmute the hurt and pain that she and her husband were going through.

In life it is not what happens to us, but how we respond, that is important. From this point of view every crisis or misfortune is an opportunity. Contained within the crisis, is the power to turn it into a blessing. There is no crisis, no matter how tragic, which cannot be transmuted into honor and achievement. The only requirement is to accept it, and offer it to God in praise and thanksgiving. Many times man has made his greatest strides during times of crisis. Usually after people have exhausted every other approach to solving a crisis they turn within and to God. This is why turning to God as a final resort is often called the "last experiment."[5] When all of the outer shells are stripped away, one faces and knows his own soul, and God.

I remember reading in the newspaper about a man who had been lost at sea for eighteen days. When his food and water ran out, he began praying. He claimed that his focusing on God, not in a pleading or begging manner to save him, but in a loving and thankful way, gave him strength and courage to survive until his rescuers came. In such situations people's lives are dramatically changed as they gain a deeper understanding of life and their relationship to it.

Being thankful is also the law of increase. What we give thanks for is automatically multiplied.[6] If we have only a dime and give thanks for it, it will soon be increased. If we resent our position and dwell upon what we lack, that is exactly what we get back. This principle can be explained this way.

There is an invisible thought-stuff on which the mind acts, making things through the operation of a law not yet fully understood by man. Every thought moves upon this invisible substance in increasing or diminishing degree. When we praise the richness and fullness of God, this thought-stuff is tremendously increased in our mental atmosphere. It reflects into everything that our mind and our hands touch.[7]

Even when we give thanks for common things, they can be transformed according to our ideals. For example, a woman living in a small town had a rag carpet in her dining room, and she had for years hoped that the carpet might be replaced with a better one. After hearing about the law of gratitude from her minister she began praising her old carpet. Greatly to her surprise, within a few weeks she was given a new carpet from an unexpected source. If this woman had resented her old carpet she would have only worsened her problem. What we resent we hold on to. When she was able to let go of the old carpet by praising it, a new one came in its place.[8]

Praise and gratitude can be used in all aspects of one's life. I know a woman who had severe headaches until she began to give thanks for them. The headaches disappeared. If you do not like your present job, give thanks for it, and you will either convert the job into a pleasant experience or praise yourself into the right job. The best way to help a child, or anyone for that matter, is to give thanks for them just as they are. They can then grow into their full potential because we have let go of the labels and boxes into which we have put them. The important thing is to stop complaining and resenting and begin to focus on the positive. By giving thanks we can begin to establish peace and harmony, first within ourselves and then in the world.

The law of gratitude is universal. It is a natural function of the soul. All things upon this earth or in the universe operate and respond to love and praise.

> All there is responds to a word of praise. God responds. We respond. Everything responds. The whole world sparkles, quivers, comes alive. Things vibrate and are quickened. We vibrate and are quickened. Heaven and earth are in tune with us, and we are in tune with them. When we give praise, everything wants to give in return.[9]

All plants and animals understand and instinctively acknowledge gratitude as the law of growth and creation. An oyster, for example, will take an irritation and turn it into a pearl.[10]

Life as seen from this level is a joyful expression of love, praise and thanksgiving instead of a hopeless struggle which eventually ends in death. Giving thanks in every circumstance, we forego the logic and reason which asks "Why me?" and open our hearts and learn to trust. Every obstacle becomes an occasion for rejoicing. We put love at the center of our universe and we are lifted beyond the world of limitation, doubt, and fear into the realm of love, hope and eternal happiness.

EIGHT

MAKING LOVE: A GIFT OF ONENESS

Marion: You are a wanton.
Robin Hood: One, I do confess,
I wanted 'til you came, but now I have you
I'll grow to embraces 'til two souls,
Distilled into kisses through our lips
Do make one spirit of Love.
BEN JONSON: THE SAD SHEPHERD

WE NOW COME to a subject both interesting and beautiful which is also one of the most abused and misunderstood aspects of human life: making love. The purpose of a sexual relationship is to become one with another human being, spiritually, mentally and physically. Man and woman are not opposites but complements to each other. If you take a right-handed glove and turn it inside out you have a left-handed glove. They are two parts of the same function. It is the same if you hold your right hand in front of a mirror; you have a left hand. Man and woman are parts of the same being. People often suggest that when you find the right person you have found your other half. It's like two halves of an apple coming together to become complete.

A sexual relationship that unites a man and a woman on all three levels (spiritual, mental, physical) requires a total giving from the heart and soul of each mate.

When the male completely gives himself to the female,

84

then she in turn can give her total energies to him and thus become one. However, if the male focuses only on the incoming energy of the female (self-gratification), it blocks his outgoing energy. The same, of course, is true for the female.

Since love is the divine governing essence of the universe, all things in life should be in accord with that essence. This includes making love which, to be truly beautiful and rewarding, should flow from the heart in love, joy and ecstasy. It is a giving, an honoring and respecting the worth of another individual's soul.

A woman in one of my classes once remarked that she had an occasional lover who was "simply a body to keep her warm at night." I told her "No one is just a body; each individual on the earth is precious and his total being must be respected." Are we not temples of the Living God? Everything on earth should be respected, considered precious or even sacred, from a blade of grass to each human soul. Pablo Casals, the greatest cellist the world has known, once became so enraptured over the beauty of a flower he wept for half an hour. This is perceiving life from your heart in its fullness and wonder. We do not necessarily have to weep over flowers, but I do think we need to hold a reverence for life and all the things that are contained within it. Life at this level is vibrant and vital, not drab or ugly. And so it is with making love.

It is wise to avoid using another person solely for you own sexual gratification. By doing so you rob this person of his or her dignity and, as another person becomes a mere object, you rob yourself of your own individual preciousness. In approaching any sexual relationship, follow the whisperings of your own heart. People often ask whether is is right for two people to use each other sexually. Two wrongs do not make a right, and it is no more right in the heart level than for one person to use another. Even marriage does not give partners the right to demand sex whenever they want it. Men and women are not objects. Even in marriage, sex needs to be right, and when it is right in the heart it is right.

There are three types of energy in sexual relations. The first is physical, the second is mental, and the third spiritual. How do each of these relate to making love?

Most people are well-acquainted with the physical aspect of sexual energy; it is something the body radiates. Often sexual relationships are built solely on the physical level. A man or a woman who is sexually frustrated may find someone solely for the purpose of releasing this energy. The two people fall into bed and have sex, but when it's over they find that's all there was. Some people remark that, afterwards, the person with whom they had sex appears very unattractive, whereas before he or she looked good. These individuals have merely used each other as objects of gratification to satisfy their own lusts. Many times they don't even want to be around each other afterwards. Most of the people involved in this type of relationship will remark about the dull aching feeling inside, because they have violated the sacredness of their souls which is a misuse of God's love.

Another aspect of sexual energy is mental. Some people use this energy, which is very powerful, to seduce others. Promiscuous people usually have strong feelings of inadequacy, coupled with a strong need for love and acceptance. By "scoring," they hope to boost their own egos in an attempt to replace what is lacking inside.

The third kind of sexual energy, the spiritual aspect of making love, concerns what goes on in the heart and soul. This divine love deep inside each of us is sensitive and delicate. When making love is right by the heart, two people become one. The spiritual substance of their hearts, their mental powers, and their physical beings unite into one and there is no separation. They become an expression of God's love to each other. This aspect of making love is fulfilling on all three planes. In this type of relationship each mate, by totally surrendering to the other, becomes balanced, renewed and fulfilled.

For centuries certain religious groups have taught a misconception about man's nature. They have said that the body is separate from the spirit or heart, so that what one does to the body does not affect the heart, and vice versa. This is simply not true. Body and spirit are one. Our bodies are hooked up to our hearts, so that what we do with the body affects the heart and what goes on in the heart is going to affect the body.

There is a trend among divorced people to sleep around for a time after the divorce. Many of the divorced people who come to the workshop have been through this experience. In talking to some of the women I found that, even though their sexual experiences were satisfactory on a physical level, their hearts have never been touched. All these people, men and women, admitted they wanted to be loved deeply in all aspects of their being.

One attractive woman remarked that she had to shut off the feelings of her heart in order to continue these affairs. But, shutting off her heart and limiting herself to physical sex, she found that she needed more and more to satisfy her and sex became like an addiction. Other women often admired her because she could shut off her heart and enjoy physical sex even though inside she knew it wasn't right, but she paid a price for it. She found herself becoming hardened, shallow and less loving. In other words, she stopped feeling. In some ways she was actually killing herself.

People who aren't living in a way that is true to themselves try to justify their actions. This woman would often tell herself "Well, everyone else is doing it, why can't I?" or "This is just an alternative lifestyle" or "I can stop any time I want." It was difficult for her to live with herself.

Since then she has found the right man and is now happy.

As she puts it, the empty chambers in her heart are now filled. When she met the right man she also realized that in her thirty-five years of life she had never been truly loved as a woman.

One day as I was giving a lecture to a group in San Francisco, a man began questioning some of the ideas about making love that I had been expressing. I asked him what he would do if he came across an attractive woman who was sexually frustrated. His eyes lit up and he said that he would probably take advantage of the situation. I replied that perhaps it might be better to look from his soul into the woman's soul and bless her (send her a lot of love) so that she would be able to find the right man. In this way she could find the deep inner satisfaction that she had been longing for. A brief sexual encounter may give momentary relief, but it really doesn't solve the problem of loneliness. I suggested that he become a true friend to this woman, help her, and not take advantage of her weakness. He agreed.

A few years ago I attended a massage workshop, but I was mistaken in thinking that it would be filled with people who wanted to learn about massage. There were twelve people present, two men and ten women, and most of them had not come to learn massage. As the day progressed I became aware of the feelings that these people were giving off. Most of these women had enough sex, but they were desperate for an honest touch. This is why they came to the workshop, to be touched. They also needed to be loved, but they did not find it there.

After the workshop I did some reflecting and found this truth. To have a truly fulfilling sexual relationship one needs to have all three elements: making love, having a loving touch, and being loved.

Motive is also important in our sexual lives. Why do we make love?

Do we use sex as an escape because we are bored with life,

or because it is difficult to talk to our sex partner? Some use sex as an ego booster, while others use another person to relieve sexual frustration. Some people use sex for revenge, punishment, or manipulation. Some use sex as a reward, or believe it is something to be earned. One man slept with a woman of another race simply to see what it was like. Someone may have many affairs in order to avoid the responsibility and depth of a one-to-one relationship.

How much more satisfying it is to make love to express to your mate some of the deepest feelings of your heart, feelings that words cannot express.

Extra-marital affairs or sleeping around are only symptoms of an unhappy heart and, probably, a relationship that isn't right. Affairs put people at odds with themselves; they can be so commonplace yet so agonizing. These affairs do not solve problems. They may give momentary relief, but in the end they only add to confusion and anguish. Some of the loneliest people are those who are having affairs or who are married to the wrong person. Being next to a person whom you really do not love or feel right about often makes the loneliness more acute. One woman remarked that her former husband had allowed her almost total freedom. She could go on ski trips alone and, even though he was unhappy about her affairs with other men, he never harassed her about it. But this did not make her happy. The pain was still in her heart. One is not free until the heart feels complete and peaceful. Happiness comes as a result of living in a way that is true to yourself.

Often couples having sexual problems will seek some type of outward cure or aid to solve their problem. It rarely works. A book on sexual techniques cannot replace what is lacking in the heart. Of course there are exceptions, but I think if the problems deep inside are solved then the outer ones melt away. One marriage counselor recommended pornography to a couple to stimulate their sex life, but the problem was their hearts, not their bodies. Anyone with a little intuition could see that this couple did not belong to each other. The husband admitted that after ten years of marriage he still didn't know or understand his wife. How can making love be good in a situation like that?

When making love is right in the heart then it's right in the mind and the body.

Since making love on these deeper levels is a gift from God—a gift of oneness, love, beauty and peace—it does not become stale or routine after five, ten, twenty or fifty years of marriage. One man who had been married for twenty-five years said his biggest thrill of the day was coming home and kissing his wife. At the heart level each kiss, caress, touch or embrace is as new and exciting as the first.

In many cases frigidity and impotence are symptoms that something is not right in a relationship; usually it is because of the absence of the right person. I know one man who stayed after class one night to talk about a "problem" he was having. After talking for about an hour he finally confessed that he was wondering whether or not he had a sex problem. He said that he had tried a brief affair but nothing happened. Because he was a sensitive and deep man I asked him whether he felt that what he had done was right. He admitted that inside it didn't feel right and I asked him how he expected to perform sexually when he knew it wasn't right in his heart. Needless to say, he was very much relieved.

I counseled a woman who had been married for eight years and thought herself to be frigid. Her husband accused her of being sexually inadequate and for years she thought something was wrong with her. She checked with doctors and psychiatrists and they could find no cause. When she took the workshop she realized that nothing was wrong with her, she just wasn't with the right man. During her years of marriage this woman had an aching or longing in her heart to be with the right man, although at the time she did not realize it.

It turned out that she is a very receptive and open person. All her life she had wanted to be with the right man and, realizing this, she was now in a position to receive the right man.

As I give lectures in various places I find more and more people listening to their hearts and following the inner voice. These people feel that making love is something to be honored and cherished. It is a gift they want to share with the right person.

Children can also be affected by their parents' sex life. Children's hearts are usually open until they are closed off by choice or by hurt, and they function most of the time on what an adult would call a meditative, or intuitive, level. Teachers sometimes have trouble in school because the child is functioning from an intuitive level while the (adult) teacher is coming from the outer, conscious level. Children pick up on thoughts and you can never lie to them. They know what is behind the words and in the heart.

If a couple is unhappy and their intimate life is reflecting that unhappiness, a child will pick up this information on an intuitive level. If a divorced parent is dating someone who is using him or her (or vice versa), the child may pick it up. The child senses that the parent is involved with someone who does not really care about the child or the parent, and sometimes develops strong feelings of rejection or resentment. Often children lose respect for the parent and their true perception of a man-woman relationship is damaged. One little boy asked his mother "How many daddies are we going to have?"

One woman who was aware of this situation refused to go out with a man who would not be a good father for her children. The next date she went on, she met the right man.

This same woman has a daughter who is bright, sensitive and open. One day they went grocery shopping. As they finished their shopping and got into the checkout lane, they passed a man who was paging through the latest male entertainment guides from a nearby magazine rack. As they stood there waiting, the little girl began to pick up on the feelings that the man was giving off as he was looking at a particular magazine. She started to shake and asked her mother what that man was doing to radiate such awful feelings.

Pornography, prostitution and similar activities have detrimental effects upon a person. People who engage in these things have to continue to find new ways of getting satisfaction. This is why more deviate ways of stimulating people have recently surfaced. Like drugs, one needs more and more perversion or non-loving stimulation to get turned on.

Making love in its truest form is a deep sharing of some of life's most intimate and precious moments. It is a celebration of life. Making love can also be a way of sharing in the successes and joys of your mate. When two people find that they are right for each other and belong together, then making love becomes an act of trust and intimacy—a trust which says "I love you" with body, mind and soul, and further, "I commit myself to this trust." An intimacy is created in which revealing or yielding their physical beings to each other also reveals the depth, love and tenderness of the lovers' inner souls. The love speaking from the depth of their hearts seeks the closeness which will make them one. There is an actual exchange of energy which makes them complete in, for and with each other.

At this level, making love expresses the joy of their love and oneness. Through this expression they honor each other and are in harmony with the universe. When two hearts have become one, deeply in love, and each person feels right with the other, making love becomes one of the most beautiful and ennobling facets of life. Making love is a gift from our Creator, a gift in which partners have the honor of surrendering in love their living temples to one another, of being one.

NINE

HOW TO FIND
THE RIGHT P ERSON

*When the one man loves the one
woman and the one woman loves the
one man, the very angels leave
heaven and come and sit in that house
and sing for joy.*

BRAHMA

*Your love shines in my heart as the
sun that shines upon the earth.*

ELEANOR DI GIULIO

IN PREVIOUS CHAPTERS we have spoken of what goes into
the right relationship and the foundation upon which it is
based. In a sense, what we have said before is only a prepara-
tion for this chapter. Our discussion has led us from the
outer levels of the conscious mind to the realm of the soul
where joy and happiness reside, and where our deepest and
most precious dreams come true. We have learned that love
and gratitude are the keys that will make us one with the universe and which have the ability or power to take negative
conditions and transmute them into love. Now we come to
the most important part of the book—how to attract and
find the right person.

Desiring to be with the right person is one of the deepest and most precious of all desires. Most of us have this desire. Some may deny it, others may ignore or rationalize it, but it is always there speaking to us, seeking the unity and oneness which makes an individual complete, happy and eternally grateful.

Since the longing to be with the right person is of the soul, it must be answered or fulfilled from the soul level. Finding the right person is not a physical seeking, nor does it require running from place to place hoping to find someone you like. It is not a mental process whereby you dwell upon the characteristics desired in a mate and then hope to attract that type of person, or one who fits into that mental pattern. It is something much deeper than that. Finding and being with the right person is moving within the realm of love and faith, which takes us into the deepest aspects of life itself.

If you are to attract the right person you must abide by the laws or principles upon which the soul functions. If the desire is to come true, the conditions set forth by the soul must be met.

For each longing in our souls there is also the promise of its fulfillment; there is never a longing without the promise of its coming true. When the conditions of the soul are met for the realization of our particular desire, it will come true. How is this done? Our dreams come true when we are willing to give them up. We must let go, or relinquish, our desire to God, placing in His hands something that is most precious to us.

One way of turning our desire over to God is through meditation. We can reach a deep level of mind by using the exercise given in Chapter 3, or by generating love for a few minutes. Once at this deep level of mind we can say a phrase which tells God of our desire to be with the right person and which will release it into His hands. The phrase that is commonly used in the workshop is:

HOW TO FIND THE RIGHT PERSON

I want to be with the right person,
the person to whom my love belongs.

The first part of the phrase, "I want to be with the right person," says that we want to be with our other half. The "right person" means that the relationship will harmonize with the spiritual essence of the universe and with our individual beings. It also says that both mates will flow together and become one, like two pieces of an interlocking puzzle. In a more mystical sense, the universe rejoices over your union, as do both of you.

"The person to whom my love belongs" concerns the heart, and can be expressed his way:

I cannot express my love for you in words,
feelings or actions; there is something
deep down inside of me that is you.

Just as the earth has its times and seasons, the stars have their place and pattern, and the world, solar system, galaxy and universe function as a harmonious whole, so does the love of two individuals who belong together.

A man or woman may sleep with another person and share meals and houses, but that doesn't make them belong. *The only person to whom your love belongs is the one to whom your love belongs.*

When two people belong, everything else seems to fall into place. The belonging flows in all areas, and making love, touching, talking, walking, being together all seem natural and beautiful. There is no uneasy silence or "wall" between them, as happens with many couples, nor is there strain or awkwardness. It just feels right being together.

True love exists between two people when their vibrations are in harmony with each other. This opens up the deepest portions of themselves, letting loose a flow of love from each of them. Because they are right for each other, acting according to divine will, they are one. When we truly seek that which belongs to us then envy disappears. There is no need to envy someone else's mate, because the right one for you will not be the right one for someone else. Each must seek his own, then happiness will follow.

Sometimes people try to make something right that isn't. Love can never be forced. You can never make another person love you. Some people have problems in relationships because they continually seek someone's love that does not belong to them. It's like trying to say that $2 + 2 = 5$, it doesn't work. When we align our will with the Will of God, then we can find our mates in a very short time and be happy.[1]

In order for the suggested meditation to work, you must give up all checklists, preconceived ideas, or images of who your mate should be. This includes wealth, social position, religion, physical and emotional characteristics, and background.

In giving up your checklists you must also be aware of conscious fantasies about who the right one will be. For several years I had a conscious fantasy about Latin American women. After I had taken a mind-awareness course, I thought I would visualize the type of woman I wanted and draw her to me. So I imagined marrying a beautiful and rich Mexican woman. I saw myself living in Mexico, enjoying all the benefits of the good life. After two months I began questioning whether this was right for me. I rationalized, telling myself "Well, it could be right, so I will continue the programming." After I moved to California I did meet a girl from Mexico who was beautiful and rich. I thought things were working out, but I introduced her to a friend and they immediately hit it off. Later she thanked me for introducing her to this man who was right for her! After that experience I promised myself I would keep my conscious mind out of the way and start listening to my inner heart.

Every person I know who has found the right person has received more than they ever dreamed of. Some have a hard time giving up their checklists or are frightened by the concept of relinquishment, but this is usually due to a faulty concept of God. Most people have been conditioned to think that God is not kind and likes to give people someone they don't like just as a sort of testing. Quite the contrary! God wants us to be happy. He wants us to be fulfilled and have our dreams come true. That is His nature.

Complete relinquishment is important. The universe cannot operate on our behalf unless we are willing to let go. Our releasing must be more than words; it must be with our hearts and souls. When we truly relinquish our longing to God, the burden of being with the right person is taken from us. All of the pain, anguish, loneliness and frustration that we are feeling is lifted from our shoulders. We are no longer anxious or desperate about finding the right person because the universe has accepted our request and it will soon by fulfilled. Thus we are given, and can feel, an inner assurance that our true mate will shortly come.

I remember talking to one woman who had taken the workshop over a year ago. She claimed that she had followed the concepts of the workshops in finding the right man, but recently she had become increasingly desperate, anxious, and even angry over not being with the right man. I asked her if she had actually released her desire and burden to God. She admitted that she hadn't and said that it seemed like such a difficult thing to do. Admittedly, at times letting go can be difficult because we must give up our self-will in the process. Often people go through so much pain and anguish that their only alternative is to release it. Sometimes we must want something so much that we are willing to give it up. However, through love and thanksgiving our releasing becomes a joyful experience, the relinquishing becomes an act of love, and our burdens are lifted from us.

Implicit in releasing our longing is an attitude of trust. We are placing in God's hands (the universe) one of our most precious and deepest desires. We are not only trusting Him with our dream but also having confidence that it will be fulfilled and that we will be happy with the mate He brings us. The late Peter Marshall illustrated this trust or lack of it with the following story.

> Suppose a child has a broken toy.
> He brings the toy to his father, saying that he
> himself has tried to fix it and has failed.
> He asks his father to do it for him.
>
> The father gladly agrees . . .
> takes the toy . .
> and begins to work.

Now obviously the father can do his work most quickly and easily if the child makes no attempt to interfere, simply sits quietly watching, or even goes about other business, with never a doubt that the toy is being successfully mended.

But, what do most of God's children do in such a situation? Often we stand by offering a lot of meaningless advice and some rather silly criticism.

We even get impatient and try to help, and so get our hands in the Father's way, generally hindering the work . .

Finally, in our desperation, we may even grab the toy out of the Father's hands entirely, saying rather bitterly that we hadn't really thought He could fix it anyway . . . that we'd given Him a chance and He had failed us.[2]

Completely releasing our heart's desire to God is an act of faith. When people have problems in finding the right person it usually means they have not given up control and are still existing on a physical or survival level. At this point the world is their source and not God.

True relinquishment is also a melting and an opening of the heart that asks that His will be done, whatever it may be. Sometimes it even means that one must be willing to receive or not receive his heart's desire.

One woman who wanted to be with the right man but also had a great fear of being alone finally, after years of pleading and begging God to be with the right man, asked,

Dear God, I now release this situation completely into Your hands. If You want me to be with the right man, that is fine, but if You want me to be alone, then I will be grateful for that. I only ask that Your Will be done.

Within three months this woman had met the right man. The point of the story is not that God did not want her to be with the right man, but her willingness to remain alone released her desire to God. Her fear of loneliness had blocked her from letting go. Many times we hold on to what we fear and to what is hurting us. In her willingness to face and live what she feared most, she banished her fear of loneliness and released her heart's desire to God. In other words, we give up our desire in order to receive it. Her surrender came when her self-effort had exhausted itself; her release was then complete.

Relinquishment is not only a way of achieving our heart's desire, but also a way of solving problems. In solving a difficulty this way, we are not working on how to solve the problem but on releasing it. It is the heart's way of solving problems. I spoke with a man who had met the right woman but the relationship was not working out. He finally realized that his own efforts to manipulate the situation were making things worse. He released the situation and asked that the right thing be done. As a result the relationship straightened out. He simply aligned himself with the universe, let go, went about his daily activities, and listened. Turning over a problem to the universe, or God, can be very helpful in any area of life.

Along with relinquishment, you must also want to be with the right person with all your heart or being. The more intense the desire, the sooner the dream will come true. There must be no conflict within our hearts; conflict or doubt will only hold us back, achieving nothing. To be sure of our desire or longing we must be honest with ourselves, and look to our God within for guidance and clarification. We need to learn to note the difference between what we truly desire in our hearts and what has been programmed into us by our environment. In sum, we must first desire to be with the right person with all our hearts and then relinquish it to the will of God. In this way all of our deepest desires and needs can be fulfilled.

How do we know we're with the right person? There is one essential ingredient. Deep within the hearts of both individuals there is a sense of belonging, a feeling of completeness and oneness. Each feels right about the other.

Couples who are right for each other find communication very easy, all the way to the soul. Simple things become joyful. I know one couple who find it enjoyable to walk to the post office together, and others like shopping or browsing in a bookstore for an evening. There is no need to keep talking all the time. They feel very comfortable being close without saying anything. There is no tension or uneasiness. One couple who had found each other were wondering whether it was really right or not. They took a trip to Canada together and that solved the problem, for they came back happier than ever. In contrast, one woman took a trip with a man about whom she had severe reservations. He thought she was the right one but she did not feel the same way. The further they got on their trip, the more uneasy she became. She knew it wasn't right. They were unable to talk and felt uncomfortable with those long silences in the car.

HOW TO FIND THE RIGHT PERSON

This feeling of belonging has to come from deep inside, not just the emotions. I once met a beautiful girl with whom I felt very compatible. We had the same ideas and goals in life, and it was even a deeply spiritual relationship, but every time I looked deep in my heart something would say "She doesn't belong to you." I would quickly shut it off, and I ended up going around with a lump in my throat for five months, which happened to be the duration of the relationship. I was trying to live a lie. After we broke up, I still found it difficult to let her go. So I finally used this phrase:

> *If you love someone*
> *Let them go,*
> *If they come back*
> *It was meant to be,*
> *If they don't*
> *It never was.*

She didn't come back. I'm very glad of that now, because of what has happened to me since. However the relationship *was* right for that time.

Another couple knew their relationship wasn't right in their hearts, but consciously they enjoyed each other's company and had a good time dating. Finally they couldn't take it inside anymore, and stopped seeing each other. Both of them have since found the right person. It was only when they admitted it wasn't right and stopped seeing each other that they found their true mates.

Another common feeling of being with the right person is that it seems to be a relationship in reverse. In the usual romance two people meet and gradually get to know each other. If after awhile they find the relationship isn't working they go and find another person. It's a hit-or-miss approach.

One woman lived with a man for a year and a half, but she knew inside it wasn't going to last. One day it simply dissolved and she left. At first she did not want any involvement with another man. Then her friends introduced her to a man they felt she *had* to meet. Immediately both of them knew it was right, but they did not want to admit it. Her subconscious programming said that she had just ended a relationship and needed to mourn for a while. Finally she stopped fighting the rightness of their relationship and got married. She remarked that they deeply loved each other at a soul level and now she had to find out who this person was. The love and depth were there from the beginning, and the other aspects of their relationship fell into place later. Even though this instant recognition doesn't happen in all cases, the main point is that the relationship feels right deep within both hearts.

When we release our heart's desire to God, we do not concern ourselves with when, how or where we are going to meet the right person. Our responsibility is to release our longing in love and gratitude and listen to God's guidance. God will arrange how, when and where we will meet our true mate. The following events happened to a man from Chicago in one month's time. On a Monday morning a man paid him a visit and offered him a job in California. Following his intuition, he accepted the job. At noon that same day his boss informed him that his job had been terminated. That same week his divorce became final, and he sold his house and moved to California. He lived in a motel for a week until he found an apartment. Two weeks later while swimming at the apartment complex pool he dove into the pool and when he came out on the other side he saw his future wife. Both of them knew immediately that they belonged together.

This man from Chicago told this story during a lunch break from my workshop. One of the class members kept asking him "How did you make those decisions?" His answer was "I didn't make any decisions; it was as though somebody upstairs was pulling the strings. All I did was listen and follow." This man added that his marriage to the right woman was one of the most beautiful and profound things that had ever happened in his life. He was deeply grateful for it.

A dear friend who lives in the Santa Cruz mountains had just ended a disastrous six-year marriage. For several years afterward he dated several women, but the experience left him unfulfilled. None of these relationships went beyond two months, and finally my friend reached a point where he could not take the frustration and anguish any longer. It seemed as though all of his energy was going into unfulfilling relationships. Late that night as he lay in bed he focused on the pain of his marriage and subsequent brief relationships and let them all go. In his releasing, he expressed a desire to be with the right woman. It didn't matter what she looked like, how much money she had, or who she was—he simply wanted to be with the right woman. His burden was lifted from his shoulders at once and he knew that the universe accepted his request. It was now just a matter of time before he met his mate.

About that same time in Los Angeles a woman was being divorced from a man to whom she had been married for ten years. After the divorce became final she felt a strong urge to move to northern California. With her few belongings and even less money she undertook the move. Several days after arriving she walked into an art store where my friend was manager. When they met they felt an immediate hook-up in their hearts, and they have been together ever since.

John Neihardt, author of *Black Elk Speaks*, met his wife this way. A woman in Paris read his book on Indian poetry and, deeply touched by the book, she wrote him a letter expressing her joy. Acting on inspiration, he responded with a letter thanking her for her comments and also proposing marriage. She accepted! It was truly a beautiful romance. He was short and she was tall but that did not hinder their love for each other. People would notice that at parties, even though they were across from each other and talking to other people, by the exchange of a slight glance they shared the depth of their love and oneness. Again, it was the oneness of their hearts and the universe which brought them together. Both Niehardt and his wife had "the courage to listen and the strength to follow." Each possessed an open and listening heart.

Many times if we are not ready to meet the right person God will help us grow into our desires. Before we can achieve any goal there are usually internal changes in the individual which are harmonious with achieving the goal. This is true in relationships. When we relinquish our desire to God, we are in a sense asking God to direct our lives. At the heart or soul level many of our habits and patterns of thinking and doing things are no longer valid. Our growing, then, is a process of letting go of all things which are not in tune with our souls. A relationship at this higher level is different than any other relationship one may have experienced. Its responsibilities, commitments and feelings go much deeper than the average romance.

Ann is one such woman who went through the experience of being prepared for the right man. At the age of twenty-two she felt a deep longing to be with the right man. After taking the workshop she realized that she must relinquish the situation to God and give up her checklist. Ann said that at first this was difficult because she had preconceived ideas of the man she wanted to be with, but after about two months she was able to completely let go of the situation. While waiting for her mate to arrive she would thank God each day for sending a man to her who would fulfill her dreams. She loved him even before she met him—each day as she drove to work she would send him her love. One day I walked into the office where she worked and she was humming a beautiful melody that I had never heard before. When I asked her what she was doing, she replied "I'm sitting here thanking

God for the right man." Her song was the gratitude flowing from her heart.

During this waiting period Ann grew emotionally as well as spiritually. One day she called and asked me to play tennis. Halfway through our practice session she stopped, walked to the net, and asked me if I thought anything was wrong with her. I answered "Not that I can think of." She said that the previous night she had gone to a cocktail party and found it difficult to deal with the empty chatter there. I offered my congratulations that she was finally beginning to grow and speak from her heart. For the next several weeks she spoke much less because she was transferring her consciousness from her intellect to her heart.

Then Ann met a man. At first she thought he was the right one, and one evening she called to tell me about him. After talking to her for a few minutes I asked her "Why do you like him?" She replied "I like his strength." "But what about him?" I asked again. Her reply was the same. She liked his mental or physical strength, not his real inner being. I realized that if she liked something *about* him, and not *him*, he probably wasn't the right man, but she would have to discover that for herself. I felt there was a lesson to be learned with this man.

After dating him a few times she discovered that in a few months he would return to New Zealand to get married, but in the meantime he wanted a lover to take care of his sexual needs. Ann refused to give in to his demands to use her in this way. She told him that she would date him as a friend only, not as a lover. When I saw Ann next she was ecstatic because she had listened to her heart and refused to be used sexually. However, dating this man proved to be a valuable growing experience. Evidently, Ann needed to clear away some negative programs before meeting the right man.

About a month later she met the right man. Both had enrolled at a swimming course at the local pool. In this class, as a swimmer progresses in skill he or she moves from lane one (beginner) to lane ten (most advanced). One day they bumped into each other in lane five. The people in their class have since referred to this meeting as "the romance of lane five." He asked her out, and after the date she went over to his apartment and never left. They have since gotten married and moved into their own house. For both it is a dream come true.

Ann's husband, Bob, is shorter than she is and is ten years older. He is very shy while she is very outgoing. In some ways they seem to be opposites, so they tend to balance each other. They are like the yin-yang principle of Eastern philosophy. During high school she was a cheerleader, graduated as valedictorian, and was one of the most popular girls in her school. Bob's background was just the opposite—he was a solitary person who liked hiking alone and was an electronics enthusiast.

In high school Ann had met a boy whom she dated for five years. He was the all-American male who was very outgoing and aggressive and who believed it was wrong to show emotion. It had been one of those on-off romances. I saw her recently and she said she is so thankful that Bob is the opposite of this former boyfriend because she realizes that Bob is what she really needed.

The last time I talked to her, Bob had just lost his job, a very lucrative one as an electrical engineer. She was ecstatic about it. She said that, with her job as a secretary, they could still make the payments on their new house (even though they would have to cut down expenses) and now Bob could find what he really wanted to do. For awhile he wanted any job that paid a high salary, but now he is looking for the job that is right for him where he will be financially successful and happy as well.

Another woman went through a ten-year marriage and had just finished a two-year relationship before she met the right man. The two-year romance had been a period of growth for her. Her true mate had been through a tragic divorce and, as he expressed it, he had to learn to walk all over again. He met her in a meditation class and knew her for over a year. Finally one night both admitted what they felt about each other and began to live together. One day I was visiting them and found that she was being sued by her bank for not paying debts left to her by the man she had been with before. She looked over to her real mate, took his hand and said "I still feel I'm one of the richest women in the world."

In growing into our desires, we are given the necessary experiences to be ready for the right person. Some people go through one or two relationships before meeting the right person—it seems to be a clearing process. One woman waited about a year to find the right man and during that time she went through a series of relationships which cleared out all the negative programming in her mind. She even had a fourteen-year-old romance revive, but only to clear itself out of the way. One individual told me that getting ready for the right person is like wiping the slate clean so a new life can be started with your true mate.

Like everything else in life, being with the right person is an opportunity for happiness and fulfillment. One woman felt she had met the right man but he refused to open his heart to her. She became quite concerned about the situation, and I told her that the relationship would come to a certain point where he would have to decide whether he loves being closed more than he loves her. We have to pay a price for being with the right person, and that price is giving up our prejudices, preconceived ideas, checklists, hates and false beliefs. What is required of us is an open heart and a willingness to listen. If this man decides to stay closed, her love will be given to another.

When one's love is given to another it is an orderly process, not chaotic or random. The universe (God) is our source and will provide us with not just anyone, but a mate who truly wants to be with us.

Sometimes people become confused over the importance of outer things. I remember in college one young man who was finishing his graduate program and wanted to find the right woman. He prayed about it and several months later he met a beautiful, wonderful girl. Both of them felt it was right, but he wouldn't accept her because he had a conscious fantasy about having a girl with skinny legs. Her legs were not quite as thin as he wished, so he broke off the relationship. Afterwards he knew that he had made a mistake. When an opportunity comes into our lives we choose either to accept and honor it or, as this young man did, reject it. The choice is ours.

One need not be afraid, because it seems that we get second chances. Sometimes two people will meet and have the opportunity of being together, but they are not ready for it, so the relationship begins a growth experience rather than the real thing. When I talk about this subject some people think that maybe a past relationship was the right one. It usually was not. When we meet the right person we know it, and there is not any doubt.

In my workshops people often ask if there is more than one right person. Not in the sense that there are many Romeos for each Juliet and many Juliets for each Romeo. Each of us is unique as an individual and there is a mate who can best fulfill our needs. Some relationships are right for a time, but being with the right person is not only something for this life but also beyond.

Again, motive is important. *Why* we do things? Many people go through life looking for substitutes to fill the empty chambers in their hearts. An actress had been raised in the theater and was on the verge of signing a long-term contract with a major Hollywood studio. As she picked up the pen to sign the contract she realized that her acting career was only a substitute for being with the right man, so she went back home and got married to her boyfriend. She is now involved in the local theater.

One word of caution. Often in life we meet people and both our hearts are open. That doesn't necessarily mean that we belong to this person, only that there is friendship involved. I've had several people become confused because they would meet a person and feel it was deep but the romance went to pieces. Admiration is the same thing—we do not want to get involved romantically with someone simply because we admire them. Only the sense of belonging and completeness makes it right.

A woman in one of my workshops said that her motto in dealing with relationships used to be "Until growth do us part." When a relationship isn't right, or perhaps is right just for a time, the partners usually grow in different directions, causing the relationship to break up. The reverse is also true: If a relationship is stagnating and neither person is growing it usually indicates the relationship is not right. I know one man who made his new wife promise that she would never change. I wonder what he was afraid of. After ten years of disappointment his wife divorced him. I counseled one woman who had an on-off relationship with a man for over three years. Each time she got back with her boyfriend she stopped growing, and she finally realized that the relationship was harming her more than it was helping her.

Obviously growth is an essential part of being with the right person, and one of the purposes why two people belong together. The idea of a true relationship says that as we grow individually we also grow together as a couple. In this case, a couple's differences made them closer and give them more to share because their hearts are one. When I met the right woman I thought our relationship would be pure bliss. I was wrong. I have never grown so much in my life, and sometimes growth is painful. One of the purposes of being with the right person is to help each other reach our true potential. As humans we sometimes have to unlearn some of the things that were put into our subconscious minds. This is necessary in order to put in the positive things and to remove the hardness from our hearts.

In some instances this growing and changing can be quite dramatic. One of the most interesting cases involves a psychic healer. At the time he met his wife he was living in Mexico. For several years he had been learning and practicing spiritual healing in Mexico City, but one day he felt very strongly in his heart that he should go to Houston. There was no logical reason why, but he had learned early in life to follow that inner voice. Fortunately, a woman he had once healed now lived in Houston. When he got there he didn't know what to do, so his woman friend set up a few lectures for him and acted as translator.

At one of the lectures he met his wife. There was almost immediate recognition that they were right for each other. Even though his future wife could not speak Spanish and he could not speak English, they felt they belonged together and they were able to communicate telepathically. They came trom different backgrounds; each had different tastes and ideas of what they consciously wanted out of life. She loved luxury and the security of an eight-to-five job. Her husband, a spiritual healer, would live where he felt God wanted him to be. Each of them had to give up their preconceived ideas of what was important and necessary in life. He had to release a dislike for the United States and she had to give up her routines and her conditioning about financial security. It has turned into an extremely beautiful relationship.

In a true relationship each mate makes an inner commitment of love to help, serve and care for the partner. This is beautifully expressed in part of the Buddhist wedding ceremony.

> MAN: *I promise to make you a success.*
> WOMAN:*I promise to make you a success.*

This means to help make that mate truly successful in all areas of life.

I think that if each of us is true to our heart we will find that there is a special reason for being on this earth, a special reason or purpose that is peculiar to that person and that will help make this world a better place to live.

There is a glorious pattern for every man's life, an individual, perfect pattern. No two people are alike, not anymore than any two plants are identical. They may be the same species, yet they are vastly different. No two leaves are alike—no two snowstorms—no two sets of fingerprints. No two lives are alike, yet each life holds a divine pattern of unfoldment, a great and holy destiny, rich in achievement and honor.

As you live true to the pattern of yourself, that deep, inner self, you will unfold as perfect, as joyous, as naturally beautiful as the tree will reach its full measure of fulfillment. No one can keep you from reaching your highest destiny if you will follow your own true pattern of life. No one can live your life for you, for only you hold the key to your own pattern of sublime, glorious, complete fulfillment.

And,

Such is the destiny written in the soul of every man and woman who comes to earth. None are without it, that completely individual highway of full expression and glorious achievement.[3]

We may discover this true purpose as we learn to listen to that inner voice; then the divine purpose will be revealed to us step by step. In most cases a couple will complement each other so that both can fulfill their purposes on this earth. And each mate helps the other in achieving their dreams.

When two people are functioning from the heart level the normal roles of man and woman or husband and wife disappear. This is not to say that their inner personalities or masculine and feminine aspects disappear, but all of the negatives which prevent them from being totally one will dissolve. Doing what is right and best for each other becomes all-important.

Many times a couple will guide, help and strengthen each other. Many times they know each other better than they know themselves.

> *I love you because*
> *When I'm with you*
> *I know and love myself.*
> *For oftimes than not*
> *Thou art my conscience.*

In this type of relationship the inner man or woman is loved. One man who was married twenty-five years had a wife who for most of this time suffered a disease which turned her body into a vegetable. But still her soul was alive and their love was deep and sincere. He never betrayed her sexually or in any other way.

Ask yourself the question: Would I still love this person if he or she could not make love? People need to be loved for themselves and not for what they can do for us.

Many years ago when my parents brought home our first television set I saw a program that impressed upon my mind the importance of loving the inner person. The story concerned a young man stationed in Germany following World War II. Joe gave his name to a club whose members wrote to lonely GIs overseas. He began to exchange letters with a young woman with whom he gradually fell in love over a period of several months. Mary's letters were deep and tender and expressed a caring and wisdom which he had not felt before. Deeply in love with Mary, he wrote and asked her for a picture of herself. She refused. However, she said that when his tour of duty ended in the next month, she would meet him in the train station in New York. She added in her letter that he would be able to recognize her by the red rose that she would be wearing in the left lapel of her suit coat.

When Joe's plane arrived in New York he immediately

went to the train station to meet his beloved. When the arrival of her train was announced he walked over by the loading platform where people would be getting off. As the train pulled in and people began to disembark his eyes searched for a woman with a red rose. At last he spotted a woman with a rose in her lapel. "Could it be Mary?" he asked himself excitedly. As he approached her he noticed that she was a woman about fifty-five, plump and very plain looking. For a moment he stood in disbelief and then asked her "Are you Mary?" The woman said "Yes, I am." Joe's mind was torn between the physical appearance of this woman and the beautiful letters that had graced their growing relationship. He thought of running and he wondered whether his love for Mary could overcome her physical appearance. And then he settled on one answer: "Yes, I still love her." He took hold of her arm and led her to a small coffee shop where they could sit and talk. After they had seated themselves a woman approached the table. She was young and attractive. She held out her hand and said, "My name is Mary. I'm the one you have been writing to." After thanking the older woman for helping her, Mary explained "I wanted to make sure your love was sincere, that you loved me and not something about me. I met this older woman on the train and asked her if she would wear this rose and say that her name was Mary. Now I think we can really get to know each other." Loving the inner person can truly make a relationship magnificent.

The emphasis on being with the right person is the giving and caring nature of the relationship. There is no criticizing, condemning or judging. There is only understanding, love, sharing and helping. It can be said this way:

> *I love you,*
> *Not only for what you are,*
> *But for what I am*
> *When I am with you,*

Not only for what
You have made of yourself,
But for what
You are making of me.
I love you
For the part of me
That you bring out;
I love you
For putting your hand
Into my heaped-up heart
And passing over
All the foolish, weak things
That you can't help
Dimly seeing there,
And for drawing out
Into the light
All the beautiful belongings
That no one else had looked
Quite far enough to find.
I love you because you
Are helping me to make
Of the lumber of my life
Not a tavern
But a temple;
Out of the works
Of my every day
Not a reproach
But a song.[4]

Being with the right person is caring for another physically, mentally and spiritually. It is caring for another's soul.

Years ago I remember reading a story about a man who had married a woman who was overweight and not very attractive physically. This man loved his wife dearly. He knew that in their love and oneness she could change into a beautiful woman. For the next five years he held a vision in his mind of his wife as a very attractive and elegant woman, and she did change into the woman he imagined. Together they accomplished something that she had been unable to do by herself. This is wanting what is best and right for our mates. This man saw the perfection in his wife—what she could become—not her faults and weaknesses.

When you find your true mate the relationship does not get old and stale. Over the years it will only grow deeper and better. As each mate changes and grows there is simply more to share. People often say "Just wait six years and watch how your relationship becomes boring." But we do not have to let what goes on in the mortal world, including the passage of time, affect our happiness. Each of us must learn from within, not without.

As the relationship grows deeper over the years each kiss is still as new and exciting as the first, each embrace is a song of ever-deepening love, and each night becomes a celebration of unity and fulfillment. Every day becomes richer and fuller.

A woman told this experience about her parents, who were in their mid-seventies when they found themselves in the hospital at the same time. Her father had been operated on a week before and was still recovering the day the doctors operated on his wife. When the nurses wheeled her back into the room they placed her on a bed next to his. Their daughter who was standing nearby saw her father try to sit up and lean over to kiss his wife, but he was unable to do so because of the tubes in his arm and nose. He lay back, but slipped his hand through the guardrails on her bed and clasped his wife's hand. He turned to his daughter and said "Have you ever seen a more beautiful woman." Their daughter later said that her parents were not just loving, they were still in love.

The poet Robert Browning and his wife Elizabeth are also examples of a love which binds two hearts into one and grows more profound and deeper with each year. Robert met

115

his wife Elizabeth Barrett in London where, as a recluse plagued by ill health, she had begun a promising career as a poet. Hearing of each other's success, both hoped for an opportunity to meet. However, when the meeting did occur, something happened that was more than the meeting of two poetic minds. Both knew that a dream had come true, a longing had been filled. Browning often mentioned to his wife that he felt they were destined to be together. Elizabeth realized this also, but sometimes wondered if such a thing were possible. Of meeting Robert, she later wrote:

> A heavy heart, Beloved, have I borne
> From year to year until I saw thy face.[5]

Elizabeth recognized that the love she felt for Robert was worth far more than wealth, fame, security, and the comforts of her father's home.

> I lived with visions for my company
> Instead of men and women, years ago,
> And found them gentle mates, nor thought to know
> A sweeter music than they played to me.
> But soon their trailing purple was not free
> Of this world's dust, their lutes did silent grow,
> And I myself grew faint and blind below
> Their vanishing eyes. Then thou didst come—to be,
> Beloved, what they seemed. Their shining fronts,
> Their songs, their splendours—better, yet the same,
> As river-water hallowed into fonts—
> Met in thee, and from out thee overcame
> My soul with satisfaction of all wants—
> Because God's gifts put man's best dreams to shame.[6]

Realizing that her tyrannical father would never permit her to marry, Elizabeth eloped with Browning to Italy. There in its sunny climate Elizabeth regained her health and became a true companion to her husband.

Awed by their own love for each other and how each year

of their marriage was better than the last, Elizabeth, writing to a relative in London, remarked "That never in his life, from his joyous childhood upwards, had he [Robert] enjoyed such happiness as he had known with me. There has not been a cloud . . ." she continued. "The only difference is from happy to happier, and from being loved to being loved more."[7] Their life was not without problems, but through their love and commitment to each other they were able to overcome them easily.

When Elizabeth died in 1861 her final words echoed again her love for Robert and the immense joy of their being together. *Immortal Lovers* records their final moments together:

On the twenty-ninth her thoughts wandered whenever she awakened from her dozing. Robert, sitting by her, watched anxiously. Now and then he spoke to her. She would then open her eyes, smile at him, and relapse into semi-consciousness. He knew she would not outlive the night. Nevertheless with Annunziata's help he tried to preserve the flickering life. Toward three in the morning, when she opened her eyes, he asked softly, "You know me?"

"My Robert—my heavens, my beloved!" she said in her ghost of a voice, reaching up and kissing him. "Our lives are held by God."

Keeping her arms about him, she repeated, "God bless you— till he laid her down gentle to sleep, for the last time, as he knew. "How do you feel?" he asked her softly.

"Beautiful!" she sighed.[8]

While living in London before her marriage to Browning, Elizabeth wrote a small book of sonnets telling of her love for him. Her favorite, "How Do I Love Thee," recounts the depth of this love.

How do I love thee? Let me count the ways.
I love thee to the depth and breadth and height
My soul can reach, when feeling out of sight

117

For the ends of Being and Ideal Grace.
I love thee to the level of every day's
Most quiet need, by sun and candle-light
I love thee freely, as men strive for Right;
I love thee purely, as men turn from Praise.
I love thee with the passion put to use
In my old griefs, and with my childhood's faith.
I love thee with a love I seemed to lose
With my lost saints,—I love thee with the breath,
Smiles, tears of all my life!—and, if God choose,
I shall but love thee better after death.[9]

Several of the Indian tribes in America had the custom of marrying two people over a running brook, one partner standing on each side of the stream. Water has always symbolized oneness, love and eternity, and in this instance the water became living water of their souls.

Being with the right person answers one of the deeper longings of the human soul. It represents the union of opposites, the fulfillment of the law of creation, and is a rare and precious gift from our Creator.

SEVEN ANSWERS

Eearlier in the book I asked you to look over seven questions, to reflect upon them, and to examine what you felt about each one in your heart. I also mentioned that by the end of the book you would have all seven questions answered. Now let's briefly go over the questions again.

1. *How does one go about finding the right person?*

The answer is very simple. In order to find and attract the right person we must relinquish our longing to God. For the releasing or letting go to work, we must also give up our conscious wills and the desire to control. In truth, we are turning over our problem to a higher will, the will of God, for an answer. We are willing to do it His way.

Dwelling upon what you want in a mate and hoping to attract that type of person to you will only lead to frustration and will not bring the inner happiness and fulfillment of being with the right person. Also, in order to relinquish our desire to God, it is necessary to give up all checklists and preconceived ideas of who the right person should be. You must even be willing to give up having your own needs fulfilled. The sooner you are able to let go completely and totally, the sooner you will meet the right person. In a sense, this process depends upon each individual's willingness to let go. With

119

some it takes quite a while; with others much less time is required.

Moreover, running from place to place will not help you to find the right person. I remember, from college days, people who would move from one apartment complex to another hoping to find the right person. Needless to say, it did not work. Attracting and being with the right person is a willingness to walk in the universe with love and trust, and to see what is there waiting for you. It is God's manifestation of love for you—His gift to you.

2. *What do you consider to be the essential characteristics of a relationship?*

Images or ideas of what goes into a relationship or what it should be like must also be given up. They are usually part of our checklists. What is essential in being with the right person is that deep sense of belonging and completeness that each mate feels for the other. Being with the right person is having an open and willing heart to do what is right for and in the relationship.

3. *What are you looking for in a mate?*

All ideas of what one wants and expects in a mate must be given up. Preconceived ideas of *who* we want in a mate only serve as stumbling blocks to finding the right person.

4. *What do you expect out of a relationship?*

Again, expectations of what we will receive from a relationship must be given up.

5. *What is communication?*

Communication is being honest with yourself and others. It is knowing and understanding that the heart is the most important aspect of an individual, and it is putting the heart first and seeing the divine within each person. In other words, communication is being able to touch and know your own heart and soul, and treating others the same way.

6. *What is love?*

Love is a universal essence which is found in and through all things. It is the basis of all life, without which there could be no happiness, or even existence.

Love is the miracle worker. It can take any heartbreak, failure, or disappointment and transmute it into honor and achievement. It can bring healing and perfection to everything it touches. Love can fulfill all of our needs whether they be of a material, mental or spiritual nature. When thinking about solving any problem or situation, think, feel, act and be Love.

7. *What is the nature of sex?*

In a true relationship making love represents oneness, completeness and joy. Each mate is a gift to the other. Making love is a manifestation of God's love and a sharing of our deepest inner selves through union of our physical beings.

TEN

VICTORY:
THE PATH OF
IMMORTALITY

I shall be telling this with a sigh
Somewhere ages and ages hence:
Two roads diverged in a wood, and I—
I took the one less traveled by
And that has made all the difference.
ROBERT FROST

WHEN TWO PEOPLE MEET, and know that deep in their hearts they belong, and realize some Greater Power than themselves has brought them together, what comes next? In a true relationship life becomes a process of helping each other to fulfill the divine purposes that each has upon this earth, to strengthen, guide and perfect one another, and to become one. With some couples this oneness is achieved very quickly. With others more time is needed. How long it takes depends upon the willingness of each mate to open the heart and listen to that inner voice, and to let go of any blocks or programs which prevent that oneness from taking place.

One couple who knew they were right for each other discovered after years of frustration that when they put God and their own hearts first, this oneness began to take place quite rapidly. Each of them had brought into the marriage

122

painful memories and false ideas of what a relationship should be. The wife had previously been married to an insensitive man who had brutalized her. Furthermore, her parents' marriage had been characterized by discord, unfilled needs and disappointment. Her husband had similar problems, although he had never been married before. He had been in several relationships which had been very painful, so he was afraid to open up completely to his wife, even though he knew she was right for him, for fear of being hurt again.

As this couple learned to open their hearts to each other, they realized that they were God's gift to one another. They also began to feel and understand that special sensitivity which enables a couple to perceive and fulfill each other on a soul level, and then manifest that same fulfillment on the spiritual and human levels. Moreover, they focused upon that divine center within and saw what each could become. They were there to help each other open their heart centers to God. They learned that the love they were expressing with each other was only an expression of divine love. In this environment they became free to be themselves and to rejoice in that freedom. There were no labels, judgments or criticisms, only a love which said "I love you for what you are, the Truth of who you are, and for what you can become."

And, coming from the pureness of their hearts, they were able to take upon themselves each other's burdens and transmute them into love, thereby nurturing each other's inner divine essence or light, which is unconditional love.

One of the most joyful and unique aspects of being with the right person is being able to see the perfection and love within one's mate, and then allowing him or her to grow into that perfection. The first Christmas that Helga and I were together I noted that as we were going through our holiday preparations she became more and more tense. She would begin winding up, like her mother, and then explode. Finally one day, after seeing her close off her heart and begin to wind up again, I walked into the kitchen, gave her a big hug, told her "I love you," and just held her. She began crying, and was then able to recognize the program she was replaying and let it go. Helga mentioned that in previous relationships she had only been criticized and condemned for acting this way. But I had an advantage. Because we were right for each other, I was able to see the difference between what was in her heart and what was going on in her mind, and to have the privilege of helping her let go of this and other programs through the gift of love.

When you gaze upon the divine center of your partner, weaknesses and faults begin falling away like old worn-out clothes. This heart or soul level is where true happiness abides. It is the realm of the great Eternal Now. Helga once attended a seminar for a week, and during some of her moments at night she reflected on what it was like being with the right man. And this is what she wrote.

> To a very special person
> To my beloved . . .
> To the source of my happiness and joy
> To the fountain of peace and love
> To my dearest lover
> To my closest mate
> To my teacher and helper
> To a friend of my soul
> To a friend of my children
> To a friend of my friends
> Whom I want to be thankful to
> Whom I want to love everyday, more and more.
> Whom I mightily adore for being so gentle,
> caring, loving, and forgiving,
>> To all of us.
>> Love, Helga

To love each other's essence and to be one—what could be more divine!

The other day I spoke with a woman who loved her husband and felt their relationship was right, but because her deep inner needs were not being met, her heart ached. After praying and meditating with me about the situation, she felt that she needed to release her husband to God and be more patient and understanding of him. After she left that evening I reflected for a moment upon her experience. I realized that what people really want and need in a relationship is that deep sense of belonging and caring, that heart-to-heart sharing, and that tenderness and understanding of each other's soul which makes one rejoice evermore. It was not that I had not known this truth before, but talking to this woman rekindled that inner knowledge. This woman already had a nice home and a good income, but these things did not matter. What she really needed was to have her inner woman and divineness loved and cherished. Wealth, fame and prestige are only substitutes for the longings and desires that people have within their hearts. Inner happiness cannot be bought, it can only come through an open and willing heart.

Being with the right person and living by that inner light is truth, beauty, happiness, joy and peace. When two people meet and know they belong, and know that God has brought them together, and then they move on to purify and perfect one another, they are glorifying God. "For in Him we live and move and have our being." In *The Apocrypha*, Christ was asked when His kingdom should come. He answered that when "the two shall be one, and that which is without shall be as that which is within." When that which is without becomes as that which is within signifies perfection, but it also means when two people shall become one, and also one in Him, then is His kingdom established. Or, "When two are gathered in My name, there shall I [Christ] be also."

NOTES

CHAPTER ONE

1. Douglas Dean, John Mihalasky, Sheila Ostrander, and Lynn Schroeder, *Executive ESP* (Englewood Cliffs, NJ: Prentice-Hall, Inc., 1974), p. 7.
2. *Ibid.*, p. 8. See also F. L. Byron, "A Top Executive's Advice: Hang Loose," Dun's Review, September 1969.
3. A list of inventions and what people thought about them, published by the American Chiropractic Association, 1975.
4. *Ibid.*
5. *Ibid.*
6. *Ibid.*
7. Edward Bono, *New Think* (New York: Basic Books, 1968), p. 5.
8. *Ibid.*, pp. 10–ll.
9. Barbara Brown, *New Mind, New Body* (New York: Harper & Row, 1974), p. 109.

CHAPTER TWO

1. Joel M. Teutsch and Champion K. Teutsch, *From Here to Greater Happiness* (Los Angeles: Price/Stern/Sloan, 1975), pp.20–21.
2. Edward W. Russell, *Design for Destiny* (New York: Ballantine Books, 1971), pp. 78–82.
3. Marianne S. Anderson and Louis M. Savary, *Passages: A Guide for Pilgrims of the Mind* (New York: Harper & Row, 1972), p. 23.

NOTES

4. Joseph Murphy, *The Miracle of Mind Dynamics* (Englewood Cliffs, NJ: Prentice-Hall, Inc., 1972), p. 37.

5. Joseph Murphy, *The Power of Your Subconscious Mind* (Englewood Cliffs, NJ: Prentice-Hall, Inc., 1975), p. 105.

6. Richard L. Evans, *Richard Evans' Quote Book* (Salt Lake City: Publishers Press, 1971), p. 203.

7. James Allen, *As a Man Thinketh* (Old Tappan, NJ: Fleming H. Revell Company), pp. 18–19.

8. Murphy, *The Miracle of Mind Dynamics.*

9. Alice Steadman, *Who's the Matter with Me* (Lakemont, GA: CSA Press, 1971), pp. 35 and 105–107.

10. Allen, pp. 15–21. See also Analee Skarin, *Ye Are Gods* (New York: Philosophical Library, 1952), pp. 34–41 and 46–55.

11. Teutsch, pp. 25–26.

12. Emile Coué, *Self-Mastery Through Conscious Autosuggestion* (London: George Allen & Unwin Ltd., 1967), pp. 22–26.

13. Coué, pp. 53–55.

CHAPTER THREE

1. Donald Curtis, *Thoughts Can Change Your Life* (Los Angeles: Wilshire Books Company, 1961), p. 27.

2. Anderson and Savary, p. 16.

3. Curtis, pp. 26–27.

4. Herbert Benson, *The Relaxation Response* (New York: William Morrow and Company, Inc., 1975), pp. 13–16.

5. This exercise is a combination of meditations from Silva Mind Control, from Buddhism, and from my own experience.

CHAPTER FOUR

1. Thomas Kelley, *A Testament of Devotion* (New York: Harper & Row, 1941), p. 29.

2. Charles Fillmore, *Dynamics for Living* (Lee's Summit, MO: Unity Books, 1967), p. 263.

3. Evans, p. 208.

4. *Ibid.*

5. J. Allen Boone, *Kinship with All Life* (New York: Harper & Row, 1954), p. 83.

6. Charles Fillmore, *Atomic Power of the Soul* (Lee's Summit, MO: Unity Books, 1968), p. 137.

CHAPTER FIVE

1. Evans, p. 173
2. John 14:10 (King James Version).
3. Skarin, pp. 140–141.
4. Jess Lair, *Hey God, What Should I Do Now?* (New York: Fawcett-Crest Books, 1973), p. 176.
5. Gordon MacDonald, *Magnificent Marriage* (Wheaton, IL: Tyndale House Publishers, 1976), pp. 35–36.
6. Stephen R. Covey, *The Spiritual Roots of Human Relations* (Salt Lake City: Deseret Book Company, 1970), pp.108–109.

CHAPTER SIX

1. Analee Skarin, *Celestial Song of Creation* (Santa Monica, CA: De Vorss & Company, 1974), p. 146.
2. John 4:7–15 (King James Version).
3 Helen Keller, *The Story of My Life* (New York: Doubleday & Co., 1954), pp. 40–41.
4. Starr Daily, *Love Can Open Prison Doors* (London: Arthur James Limited, 1974), pp. 13–14.
5. Skarin, *Ye Are Gods*, p. 262.
6. Frank S. Mead, ed., *The Encyclopedia of Religious Quotations* (New York: Pillar Books, 1976), p. 222.

CHAPTER SEVEN

1. Merlin Carothers, *Power to Praise* (Plainfield, NJ: Logos International, 1972), p. i.
2. Skarin, *Ye Are Gods*, pp. 137–140.
3. Catherine Marshall, *Something More* (New York: Avon Books, 1976), p. 31.

NOTES

4. Napoleon Hill, *You Can Work Your Own Miracles* (Greenwich, CT: Fawcett Publications, Inc., 1971), pp. 100–104.

5. Daily, p. 15.

6. Analee Skarin, *Temple of God* (Santa Monica, CA: De Vorss & Company, 1958), p. 113.

7. Fillmore, *Dynamics for Living*, p. 229.

8. *Ibid.*, p. 230.

9. James Dillet Freeman, *Prayer: The Master's Key* (New York: Doubleday & Company, Inc., 1968), p. 136.

10. Steadman, inside cover.

CHAPTER EIGHT

1. Eugene A. Albright, *Uni-Chotometrics: A New Way of Life* (Detroit, MI: Harlo Printing, 1967), pp. 135–136.

CHAPTER NINE

1. Analee Skarin, *To God the Glory* (Santa Monica, CA: De Vorss & Company, 1956), p. 62.

2. Catherine Marshall, *Beyond Ourselves* (New York: Avon Books, 1968), pp. 98–99.

3. Skarin, *Ye Are Gods*, pp. 22–23.

4. Cecelia Reed, *A Gift of Love* (New York: Bantam Books, 1977), pp. 22–23.

5. Elizabeth Barrett Browning, *Sonnets from the Portuguese* (New York: Harper & Row), p. 25.

6. *Ibid.*, p. 26.

7. Francis Winwar, *The Immortal Lovers* (New York: Harper & Brothers, 1950), pp. 202–3.

8. *Ibid.*, pp. 280–81.

9. Browning, p. 43.

BIBLIOGRAPHY

Albright, Eugene. *Unichotometrics: A New Way of Life.* Detroit, MI: Harlo Printing, 1967.

Allen, James. *As A Man Thinketh.* Old Tappan, NJ: Fleming H. Revell Company.

Anderson, Marianne S. and Savary, Louis. *Passages: A Guide For Pilgrims of the Mind.* New York: Harper & Row, 1972.

Bono, Edward. *New Think.* New York: Basic Books, 1968.

Boone, J. Allen. *Kinship With All Life.* New York: Harper & Row, 1954.

Brown, Barbara. *New Mind, New Body.* New York: Harper & Row, 1974.

Browning, Elizabeth Barrett. *Sonnets from the Portuguese.* New York: Harper & Row.

Carothers, Merlin. *Power to Praise.* Plainfield, NJ: Logos International, 1972.

Covey, Stephen R. *The Spiritual Roots of Human Relations.* Salt Lake City: Deseret Book Company, 1970.

Coué, Emile. *Self-Mastery through Conscious Auto-Suggestion.* London: George Allen & Unwin Ltd., 1967

Daily, Starr. *Love Can Open Prison Doors.* London: Arthur James Limited, 1974.

Dean, Douglas, Mihalasky, John, Ostrander, Sheila, and Schroeder, Lynn. *Executive ESP.* Englewood Cliffs, NJ: Prentice-Hall, Inc., 1974.

BIBLIOGRAPHY

Evans, Richard L. *Richard L. Evans Quote Book.* Salt Lake City: Publishers Press, 1971.

Fillmore, Charles. *Atom-Smashing Power of Mind.* Lee's Summit, MO: Unity Books, 1968.
_____. *Dynamics for Living.* Lee's Summit, MO: Unity Books, 1967.
Freeman, James Dillet. *Prayer: The Master Key.* New York: Doubleday & Company, Inc. 1968.

Hill, Napoleon. *You Can Work Your Own Miracles.* Greenwich, CT: Fawcett Publications, Inc. 1971.

Keller, Helen. *The Story of My Life.* New York: Doubleday & Company, 1954.
Kelley, Thomas. *A Testament of Devotion.* New York: Harper & Row, 1941.

Lair, Jess. *I'm Not Much, Baby, But I'm All I've Got.* New York: Fawcett, 1978.
Lair, Jess, and Lair, Jacqueline. *Hey, God, What Should I Do Now?* New York: Fawcett-Crest, 1978.

MacDonald, Gordon. *Magnificent Marriage.* Wheaton. IL: Tyndale House Publishers, 1976.
Marshall, Catherine. *Beyond Ourselves.* New York: Avon Books, 1968.
_____. *Something More.* New York: Avon Books, 1976.
Mead, Frank, ed. *The Encyclopedia of Religious Quotations.* New York: Pillar Books, 1976.
Murphy, Joseph. *The Power of Your Subconscious Mind.* Englewood Cliffs, NJ: Prentice-Hall, Inc., 1975.

Reed, Cecelia. *A Gift of Love.* New York: Bantam Books, 1977.
Russell, Edward W. *Design for Destiny.* New York: Ballantine Books, 1971.

Skinn, Florence Scovel. *The Game of Life and How to Play It.* New York: Gerald J. Rickard, 1941.

Skarin, Analee. *Celestial Song of Creation.* Santa Monica, CA: De Vorss & Company, 1974.
_____. *Temple of God.* Santa Monica, CA: De Vorss & Company, 1958.
_____. *To God the Glory.* Santa Monica, CA: De Vorss & Company, 1956.
_____. *Ye Are Gods.* New York: Philosophical Library, 1952.
Steadman, Alice. *Who's the Matter with Me?* Lakemont, GA: CSA Press, 1971.

Teutsch, Joel, and Teusch, Champion. *From Here to Greater Happiness.* Los Angeles: Price/Stern/Sloan, 1975.

Winwar, Francis. *The Immortal Lovers.* New York: Harper & Brothers, 1950.